MW01061712

"For centuries the world's c
heart. Finally we have a sin
do it. Impeccable scientific
about the truth of who we ¿
niques done consistently over time can transform not only our own lives, but the
whole world. I'm not exaggerating when I say *Heart Intelligence* should be
required reading for everybody on the planet."
— **Jack Canfield, Coauthor of** *The Success Principles*™ **and the NY Times #1
Bestselling** *Chicken Soup for the Soul®* **series**

"*Heart Intelligence* is a wonderful exploration of the science of the deeper heart
and why we should learn to listen to it. This book is required reading for anyone
who wants to get their heart and head working together to create and *not wait*
for their fulfillment."
— **John Gray, Bestselling Author of** *Men Are from Mars, Women Are from Venus,*
and *Venus on Fire, Mars on Ice*

"The HeartMath Institute has done it once again! By using science as the
contemporary language of mysticism, they have elegantly married age old wisdom and spirituality with their latest cutting-edge research and then they provide us with the practical tools to begin our own journey into heart intelligence.
This book is an impeccable representation of what we all innately believe to be
true. The brain may think, but the heart knows."
— **Dr. Joe Dispenza, NY Times Bestselling Author of** *You Are the Placebo:
Making Your Mind Matter* **and** *Breaking the Habit of Being Yourself: How to Lose
Your Mind and Create a New One.*

"Doc Childre and the HeartMath team have written a powerful book from a
place of deep love and care for people. They offer profound insights to access
the intuitive intelligence we each need to make our highest choices during these
changing times. I believe *Heart Intelligence* will make a big difference in the lives
of many people."
— **Lynne Twist, Co-founder, The Pachamama Alliance, author of the award-
winning book** *The Soul of Money*

"This book is destined to help many people learn how to live from their heart's
intuitive guidance to connect the puzzle pieces of their purpose and fulfillment.
I love HeartMath and have used its methods to connect with my intuitive heart
with great success. In fact, learning to listen to and follow my heart has been
the secret to my success."
— **Marci Shimoff, #1 NY Times Bestselling Author,** *Happy for No Reason, Love For
No Reason,* **and** *Chicken Soup for the Woman's Soul*

"*Heart Intelligence* is a fascinating, powerful way to learn how to relieve stress and improve the overall health of your mind and body. I highly recommend it."
— **Daniel Amen, MD, author of the NY Times Mega Bestseller *Change Your Brain, Change Your Life.***

"*Heart Intelligence*, is an informative work and an excellent resource to use as a compass in divining the path of your life."
-**Bruce Lipton, Ph.D., author of *The Honeymoon Effect* and of the bestseller *Biology of Belief*.**

"*Heart Intelligence* is a must read for those wanting to enrich their own lives and our shared experience of life. It unlocks the wisdom and potential within all of us to transform our personal lives, our relationships and the future through profound heart and mind connections. Buy this book for yourself and give copies to those you care about."
— **Simon Mainwaring, CEO We First, author of *We First***

"Between these covers lies the key to resilience in times of change, uncertainty, and stress. *Heart Intelligence* is a must read."
— **Barnet Bain, director *Milton's Secret* (Eckhart Tolle movie to be released fall 2016), producer *What Dreams May Come*, author *The Book of Doing and Being*.**

"*Heart Intelligence* is a must read! For bio-hackers, performance junkies or anyone interested in a better life, the ideas in the book are critical."
— **Steven Kotler, NY Times Bestselling Author of *The Rise of Superman, Bold and Abundance*.**

"*Heart Intelligence: Connecting with the Intuitive Guidance of the Heart* encourages us to roll our sleeves up and do what we feel we already know but are too busy to give attention to. This informative book teaches us how to connect with our heart's intuitive guidance *moment-to-moment* to make better choices *even* in the middle of challenging situations. It's a must read."
— **Dr. Ivan Misner, BNI Founder & NY Times Bestselling Author**

"*Heart Intelligence: Connecting With the Intuitive Guidance of the Heart* is a concise handbook for heart-based living. In a conversational style that's easy-to-read, the authors lead us on a journey of empowered living — for us, our families, our communities, and ultimately, for our world. From engineers to homemakers, from politicians to healers, *Heart Intelligence* gives new meaning to the role of your heart—while awakening the deep intuition that can empower the best choices you will ever make. I love this book!"
— **Gregg Braden, NY Times Bestselling Author of *The Divine Matrix* and *Resilience From The Heart***

HEART INTELLIGENCE

**Doc Childre, Howard Martin,
Deborah Rozman and Rollin McCraty**

Waterfront Press

HeartMath, Quick Coherence, emWave and Heart Intelligence are registered trademarks of Quantum Intech, Inc. Inner Balance is a trademark of Quantum Intech, Inc. Heart Lock-In, Freeze Frame and Freeze-Framer are registered trademarks of the Institute of HeartMath. TestEdge is a registered trademark of Heart-Math LLC.

iPhone, iPod Touch and iPad are registered trademarks of Apple Inc. Other company and product names may be trademarks of their respective owners.

ISBN: 978-1-943625-43-7 PRINT
ISBN: 978-1-943625-42-0 EBOOK

Published by Waterfront Press
www.waterfrontdigitalpress.com

DEDICATION

This book is dedicated to the increasing numbers of people who are feeling a desire for a deeper connection with their heart. Our mission at HeartMath is to help people bring their physical, mental and emotional systems into coherent alignment with their heart's intelligent guidance system. The guiding voice or feelings of the heart have been referred to in writings and teachings throughout millennia. Unlocking this inner guidance can enable us to navigate through these changing times with more personal balance, coherence and heart-based connection with each other. This connection can help shift humanity's energies from separation to cooperation resulting in higher solutions to our global problems. We feel that establishing a partnership between our mind and heart, along with expanding our love, kindness and compassion, will become the new baseline for creating the world as we want it to be. Our research and tools are dedicated to simplifying this process, in cooperation with like-hearted others who hold important pieces of the puzzle.

CONTENTS

CHAPTER 1

IT'S HEART TIME

By Howard Martin

Most of us feel that our lives keep speeding up. That's actually been going on for a while. It's just going faster now than ever before—more to do in less time, more things pulling us in different directions. It's easy to feel relentlessly bombarded with "high-speed" communications and an overload of information. New technologies designed to make things happen more quickly seem to be quickening us on the inside too. It's often hard to keep up. One word describes what many of us frequently feel—Overwhelmed.

However, another momentum is also taking place. Many people from different backgrounds, cultures and professions are sensing an impetus for positive change within themselves and in the world. There is an inner stirring, a prompting from our intuition to awaken to new possibilities and a desire to grow. When I speak to audiences all over the world, I observe people responding to these inner promptings and making changes in the most elegant and beautiful ways. They are taking action on their insights, shifting beliefs and values, overcoming old patterns, accepting and embracing change and making an effort to facilitate the larger whole.

The increasing complexity we experience in modern life is an outward reflection of the speed of change. Life, including each of us, is always evolving. It is just happening at a very fast pace now, during an important and unique time in history. Old systems are dying and new ones are trying to emerge. Numerous societies and governments are in a state of rapid, often chaotic transformation. Faster change and growth seem to be the evolutionary imperatives of our time.

One of the most important aspects of the changes taking place is the emergence of a more heart-based awareness or "heart intelligence." Learning to access the heart's intelligence is a key to managing the speed of personal and planetary change while creating a new life experience of increased fulfillment. Throughout this book we will explore heart intelligence, what it is, the scientific research on it, how we can develop it and what can happen as more and more people awaken to this powerful resource that lives within us all.

In the workshops I give, people often share their challenges trying to manage so much change taking place in such a short amount of time. They also share a deep sense of opportunity to help usher in a new and very different world, and the realization that we have to do it together. I am often asked questions such as: How can we advance individual and collective growth and improve the state of the world? How do we handle so much change and maintain balance? How can we use this momentum of change to find new fulfillment in life? How can we find solutions to problems that seem to have no viable solutions? What can I/we do? In the forty plus years I've spent focusing on my own personal development, I found that my answers to questions such as these have come from a deep place in my heart, not from mental speculations.

I have been fortunate. When I was a young man I had a realization that life was about continuous growth and I felt my life had to be about service to others in some way. While it was exciting to have these insights, it was also a bit disconcerting. I was overly ambitious, full of myself and prone to the pitfalls most of us experience as we mature. I pondered how I could stay committed to my growth, make changes I knew I needed to make and not become complacent. I wondered how I could overcome the resistances, vanities and self-centeredness I had, as well as the growth challenges life can present while trying to find practical, meaningful ways to serve others.

Through pursuing the path with friends and the promptings of life, I began to see that my way forward was through the conscious development of qualities born from what I understood as "heart," such as care and compassion, and replacing judgmental reactiveness with more kindness. My heart's promptings cultivated a genuine desire to become a self-empowered person and to find ways to live that were more balanced, loving and fulfilling. Following those heart promptings eventually led me to work with Doc Childre and others to help unfold the HeartMath system that Doc was creating.

The development and growth of HeartMath has far exceeded any vision I could possibly have had when we started. That realization alone is something for me to always appreciate. It is verification that life can exceed expectations when I listen to and follow my heart. The practice of unfolding my heart intelligence is what has given me the sustained motivation to stay true to my commitments and put me in a position where I can help others learn how to do this as well.

Simply put, HeartMath is a system for awakening and developing our heart's intelligence. It includes heart-based tools designed to help people empower, to connect with their heart's intuitive guidance and unlock the potential of who they really are. We share the HeartMath system through books, technologies and training programs that have been delivered to thousands of individuals interested in personal growth or improving their health and performance. HeartMath has worked with Fortune 500 companies, health care systems and social service sectors, such as educational institutions, the military and law enforcement. Through this process, millions of lives have been touched. We have learned a lot about people, and especially ourselves, some of which we will share in these writings.

As you will find in the coming chapters, science has always played a big role in HeartMath. Long before the HeartMath organizations were officially formed, Doc realized that if we were going to offer a system called "heart intelligence," we needed a bridge to take the philosophical and spiritual understanding of heart into practical day-to-day applications. He chose science as one of the building blocks of that bridge.

When something is better understood through scientific research, it increases the power of belief and application. Many people want to believe in and trust their hearts more, but often don't know the difference between what their heart is saying and their mental or emotional biases. If scientific research could reveal new understandings about the heart, emotions and mind, it would make it easier for people to accept and apply what they already intuitively know and feel.

In the early 1990s the HeartMath Research center was established, and since that time it has greatly expanded people's understanding of the heart's role beyond being an organ that pumps our blood. In forthcoming chapters you will see that the heart is also an information processing center that sends important information throughout the body and can have profound influences on our brain. In the lab, our researchers started by looking at the physiological connection between emotional state, the heart and the brain. They found that a measurement called Heart Rate Variability (HRV) was reflective of people's emotional states and that HRV or heart rhythm analysis offers a unique window into the communication between the heart, brain and emotions.[1] Over the years, the HeartMath research lab became one of the leading authorities in this field.

Researching HRV helped us refine techniques to improve heart/brain communication and to self-generate a highly beneficial physical and emotional state called physiological coherence, or "heart coherence" for short. We found that positive feelings of love, care, appreciation and other uplifting emotional qualities long-associated with "heart" activated this state of coherence. This important discovery on the link between emotion and the heart's rhythms was published in the *American Journal of Cardiology* in 1995 and then in other peer-reviewed scientific journals.[2] Further studies on how people can learn to activate heart coherence led to the development of our HRV technology products (originally Freeze-Framer®, then emWave® and Inner Balance™ Trainer), which by now have been used by people in over 100 countries as a way of training themselves to improve their emotional self-regulation and self-empowerment skills.

Social science has also played a role in our research. We created pre- and post- assessments to determine the effectiveness of our programs in organizations, health care and education. As people practiced Heart-Math methods, there were significant results in lowered stress levels, improved health, reduced health care costs, improved test scores, and heightened ability to sustain positive emotional states, along with other performance measures. Increased heart coherence also resulted in a deeper connectedness between people. Researchers recorded a number of instances in which a loving mother's brain waves synchronized to her baby's heartbeats and where happy couples' heart rhythms synchronized with each other when sleeping together.[3] They also found that increased physiological heart coherence in individual team members resulted in enhanced synchronization and performance—a type of team coherence.

Anyone who has watched a championship sports team or experienced an exceptional concert knows that something special can happen in a group that transcends their normal performance. It seems as though the players are in sync and communicating on some unseen energetic level. Many teams, including

Olympic and professional sports teams, understand the importance of team coherence. While they may refer to coherence as "team spirit" or "bonding," they instinctively know there is a palpable "team energy" that impacts their performance. Such elite teams pay close attention to their group's cohesion, and the team leaders actively take steps to resolve any interpersonal conflicts or distortions that may hinder or erode it. They know that internal group discord or conflict has a negative impact on the team. They also know it takes connecting with the power of the heart to create team coherence.

Curt Cronin, CDR (SEAL) former Commander Navy Seal Team Six and his partner Dr. Jay Ferraro, PhD, are HeartMath Certified Trainers who work with NFL players and teams using HeartMath techniques with emWave HRV technology to help them connect with the power of the heart and monitor their heart rhythms to develop team coherence. Here is great story that illustrates what can happen when a higher level of team coherence occurs. It was taken from the book, *Second Wind: The Memoirs of an Opinionated Man* written by basketball legend Bill Russell.

"Every so often a Celtics game would heat up so that it became more than a physical or even mental game, and would be magical. That feeling is difficult to describe, and I certainly never talked about it when I was playing. When it happened, I could feel my play rise to a new level. It came rarely, and would last anywhere from five minutes to a whole quarter, or more. Three or four plays were not enough to get it going. It would surround not only me and the other Celtics, but also the players on the other team, and even the referees.

"At that special level, all sorts of odd things happened: The game would be in the white heat of competition, and yet somehow I wouldn't feel competitive, which is a miracle in itself. I'd be putting out the maximum effort, straining, coughing up parts of my lungs as we ran, and yet I never felt the pain. The game would move so quickly that every fake, cut, and pass would be surprising, and yet nothing could surprise me. It was almost as if we were playing in slow motion. During those spells, I could almost sense how the next play would develop and where the next shot would be taken. Even before the other team brought the ball inbounds, I could feel it so keenly that I'd want to shout to my teammates, 'it's coming there!'—except that I *knew everything would change if I did. My premonitions would be consistently correct, and I always felt then that I not only knew all the Celtics by heart, but also all the opposing players, and that they all knew me. There have been many times in my career when I felt moved or joyful, but these were the moments when I had chills pulsing up and down my spine.*

"... On the five or ten occasions when the game ended at that special level, I literally did not care who had won. If we lost, I'd still be as free and high as a sky hawk."

Most all of us have had the experience of walking into a room and feeling immediately uplifted by the positive vibration of the people there, and at another time walking into a room and sensing that people's feelings were at odds with each other although everyone appeared fine. What we were experiencing was some type of heart-to-heart bio-communication or energetic transfer. To research this, the HeartMath team wanted to see if they could detect heart-to-heart bio-communication between a person and their pet.[4] They looked at the heart rhythms of a twelve-year-old boy, Josh, and his dog, Mabel, using two portable HRV recorders, one fitted on Josh and the other on Mabel.

They synchronized the recorders and placed Mabel in one of our labs. Josh then entered the room and sat down a few feet away from Mabel and proceeded to consciously radiate feelings of love towards the dog. In the graph below, note the synchronous shift to increased coherence in the heart rhythms of both Josh and Mabel as Josh consciously radiated love to his dog. An energetic transfer was taking place through their emotional connection. The graph was like a signature that reflected the love and bonding that was taking place.

The research lab did a similar experiment with a woman named Ellen and her horse, Tonopah, and saw the same synchronous shift to increased coherence in Ellen and her horse. This occurred while Ellen was practicing HeartMath's Heart Lock-In® Technique and sending love to Tonopah (see graph next page) from just inside the corral. Again both Ellen and her beloved horse were linked in some unseen way.[4]

A Boy and His Dog
(Heart Rhythms)

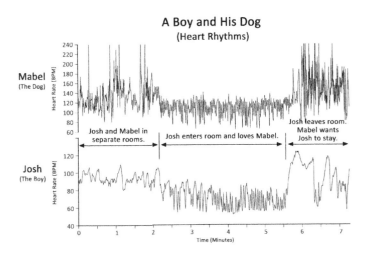

Mabel
(The Dog)

Heart Rate (BPM)

Josh
(The Boy)

Heart Rate (BPM)

Josh and Mabel in separate rooms.

Josh enters room and loves Mabel.

Josh leaves room. Mabel wants Josh to stay.

Time (Minutes)

Ellen and Her Horse

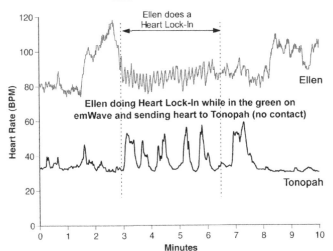

Ellen does a Heart Lock-In

Ellen

Heart Rate (BPM)

Ellen doing Heart Lock-In while in the green on emWave and sending heart to Tonopah (no contact)

Tonopah

Minutes

13

When I show these slides in my presentations, people in the audience sometimes start to tear up a little. It touches something deep inside the heart. I know it did with me the first time I saw the graphs. From this research, we can see that as people practice heart coherence, it generates an energetic field that makes it easier for others to connect with their heart and create social coherence.

Today much of our research is focused on the science of interconnectivity. Our vision is to help create a more heart-connected world and to explore the potential of global coherence. It's well-documented that humans and animals are affected by changes in the earth's magnetic (energetic) fields. The research team is testing the hypothesis that humanity is actually interacting with the earth's magnetic fields. Thus far, our research studies have found that the heart rate variability (HRV) or heart rhythms of individuals in different locations across the planet actually synchronized with each other over a 30-day period, indicating humanity is synchronized to rhythms in the earth's fields. (We will talk more about exciting social and global coherence research later in this book.)

Emerging Heart Awareness

There is much more to the emergence of new heart awareness than what HeartMath science or anyone's science has contributed so far. It's in the air. More speakers, articles, books and programs are referring to the heart. More company mission statements make a point to mention the importance of the heart in leadership and customer care. Whether people mention speaking from the heart, listening to the heart, connecting with the heart or following the heart, it is a clear sign that there is an increased energetic awareness of the importance of the heart in life's decisions.

I have been seeing more references to the heart and qualities associated with the heart in areas I wouldn't have imagined. For example, in advertising and business. Whether or not it is a motivation to sell more products, advertisers are more overtly using words and images related to heart with messages about love, care and compassion. "Purpose Driven Marketing" and "Conscious Capitalism" are examples of heart-based movements that are changing how business is done.

A new understanding of "heart" that moves past just the philosophical, often soft characterization is advancing into a realization of the heart as a dynamic, connecting, creative intelligence. Connecting the physical, emotional, intuitive and spiritual aspects of heart in a coherent alignment can lead to a new way of perceiving, thinking, acting and relating—which we call heart-based living.

The purpose of this book is to provide an understanding of heart intelligence and how to apply it in practical ways to raise our vibration which enables us to manage our energy, unfold our higher potentials and create a fulfilling life. We will be sharing key practices and concepts, some of which may be new to you and others you may have explored along your own personal path. We will expand on the benefits of learning to access our heart's discernment and guidance to create forward movement through these transformational times with much more clarity, ease and grace.

Of course paradigms don't change overnight, but as the planetary heart energetics increase and we gain more understanding of heart intelligence, we will collectively refine and advance the process. As I travel in the U.S., Europe and Asia, I see people from many different occupations increasingly demonstrating the qualities of heart-based living. It's hard to quantify, but amidst the conflicts and struggles taking place I perceive new awareness and hope manifesting. It shows up in casual, uncalculated moments. There is often a different quality in how people communicate with one another, demonstrated by a spirit of openness, general respect and collaboration. I observe a new alignment with core values that people are using to guide their decisions and actions. It is especially evident in the ways that people react or don't react to challenges. The normal, predictable, emotional patterns just don't seem to be as dominant at times.

The next few paragraphs are some of Doc's thoughts on the planetary shift we are experiencing that helped explain to me what I was seeing.

"Even as the world is becoming more heart-connected, it is also obvious that the global stress bar is being raised. Waves of emotional turbulence modulate throughout the planet, resulting from our collective emotional responses to terrorism, wars, climate change swings of droughts, floods, tornados and other

Earth changes, world stage instability, and on. These stress waves get powerfully stirred and amplified by the media, which sustains a collective uneasiness that can dampen how we think, feel and respond to life's interactions—especially on the emotional level.

"On the upside, the media and internet provide us with a world view that is drawing out more love, care and compassion for humanity's challenges than we've ever experienced at one time on the planet. This influence is showing up in the thousands of social causes that continue to form through the internet connectivity available today. More people are caring and taking action in areas of global challenge like social and financial inequities, healthcare and political reform, ecology and much more. The people's voice, the voice of their hearts, is rising and increasingly being heard. People in every part of the world regardless of culture, age, spiritual/religious beliefs and so on are experiencing an up-grade in heart-based awareness.

"As more people access their heart's intelligence, it creates an energetic connection that makes it easier for others to do the same. We contribute to this energetic momentum of heart-based awareness as we take responsibility to release judgments and separation.

This helps to clear the energetic density between our spirit and humanness that restricts the manifestation of our higher potentials. It requires self-empowerment and there is more facilitation and capacity to do that now than ever. As time unfolds, the general tone of collective consciousness will progressively change from survive to thrive as humanity becomes kinder, more compassionate and cooperative through this transformational adventure."

It's an adventure in discovering the power of the heart.

1.   McCraty, R., Atkinson, M., Tomasino, D., & Bradley, R. T, The coherent heart: Heart-brain interactions, psychophysiological coherence, and the emergence of system-wide order. Integral Review, 2009. 5(2): p. 10-115.

2.   McCraty, R., et al., The effects of emotions on short-term power spectrum analysis of heart rate variability. Am J Cardiol, 1995. 76(14): p. 1089-93.

3.   McCraty, R., The energetic heart: Bioelectromagnetic communication within and between people, in Bioelectromagnetic Medicine, P.J. Rosch and M.S. Markov, Editors. 2004, Marcel Dekker: New York. p. 541-562.

4.   McCraty, R., The Energetic Heart: Biomagnetic Communication Within and Between People, in Bioelectromagnetic and Subtle Energy Medicine, Second Edition, P.J. Rosch, Editor 2015.

CHAPTER 2

ATTRIBUTES OF HEART INTELLIGENCE
By Deborah Rozman

"Picture heart intelligence as the flow of awareness, understanding and intuitive guidance we experience when the mind and emotions are brought into coherent alignment with the heart. This intelligence steps down the power of love from universal source into our life's interactions in practical, approachable ways which inform us of a straighter path to our fulfillment."

– Doc Childre

There are many aspects to heart intelligence that we'll touch on from different angles throughout this book. Most people reference their heart as something more than just their physical heart. When I was teaching meditation to children in a public school classroom of seven year olds, I asked them, "Point to your real self," and everyone in the class pointed to their heart. They naturally felt their heart was who they really are. Regardless of race, religion or ethnicity, throughout history people have referred to their heart as their source of being, intuition and wisdom. In most every language, we find metaphors of the heart like, "listen to your heart," "go to your heart for the answer," or "put your heart into it." Many ancient cultures, including the Mesopotamians, Egyptians, Babylonians and Greeks referred to the heart as a source of *intelligence*. They maintained that the heart is the primary organ capable of influencing and directing one's emotions, morality and decision-making ability, so they consequently attached enormous emotional and moral significance to its behavior. Over thousands of years, most often without knowing about one another, cultures across the planet seemed to share a similar knowledge about the *heart* as a source of intelligence and inner guidance.

From my personal experience teaching Gestalt psychology to adult classes in the early 1970s, I realized that the head and the heart were two different intelligence systems. There was nothing that I could find in the psychological literature at that time that could explain what I was observing. When a student was in conflict about a relationship or career issue, I would place two pillows on the floor and have the student pretend one pillow was the head and the other pillow was the heart. I would have students sit on the head pillow and have their head talk to their heart. After sharing their thoughts and concerns, I'd have them move to the heart pillow and tell their head what their heart's view of the problem was and what their heart was feeling. It was often like two different people talking from two different reference points of awareness. Then I'd have them go back to the head pillow and respond to their heart. After switching pillows in this way 3 or 4 times, they'd settle in their heart and speak from their heart's wisdom. What occurred was an obvious shift in the depth of what they would say and a different energetic quality that was palpable to them and the whole class. The intuitive insights that emerged from bringing their head and heart together resulted in a solution to their conflict or a clear next step. I witnessed this so many times I was convinced that the heart was accessing a source of intelligence.

When I met Doc Childre in the mid 1980s and heard him talk about "heart intelligence," I immediately knew what he meant, though I wasn't familiar with the term. He invited me and others to help create an institute to explore heart intelligence through research. I

accepted the offer with enthusiasm because it reso-
nated with my past studies and experience with the
heart.

As we started our research we asked ourselves,
"Are the spiritual and physical heart connected in any
measurable way? Is what people refer to as heartfelt
emotions just an aspect of the brain or is the physical
heart involved in emotional experience? Is it involved
in intuition?" These are some of the queries we pondered as we formed the HeartMath research center in
the early 1990s. It was important to understand how
the heart and brain communicate and to investigate
the heart's role in emotional experience, intuition and
self-regulation. So we formed a scientific advisory
board of esteemed brain researchers, cardiologists,
psychiatrists, psychologists, physicists and engineers
who were all interested in researching any connection
between the physical heart and the spiritual heart.

Our research began with exploring the latest findings in the fields of neuroscience, neuro-cardiology,
psychology, physiology, biochemistry and biophysics.
In synthesizing research from these different disci-
plines, it was surprising to discover that the physical
heart sends information to the brain and body through
at least four different pathways: a neurological com-

munication system (through ascending pathways in the autonomic nervous system); bio-physical communication (the pulse wave); biochemical messaging (the heart secretes a number of hormones); and, through the electromagnetic field created by the heart.[1] We also discovered that what we *feel* influences and is influenced by the activity of the physical heart and that our *feelings* are a key aspect to unlocking "heart intelligence."

Understanding Intelligence

The word intelligence comes from the Latin verb *intelligere* which means to "pick out" or discern. This term "intelligence" has a long history of being linked to metaphysical ideas, including theories of the immortality of the soul.[2] However, exploring "intelligence" was relatively uncommon until the early 1900s. Since then, intelligence has been described in many ways, including our abilities for abstract thought, understanding, self-awareness, communication, reasoning, learning, having emotional knowledge, memory retention, planning, problem solving and more. It's interesting that as human awareness has evolved, so have our discernments on what intelligence is.

Today, there are numerous definitions of intelligence by scholars with no real consensus. Within many circles, intelligence has been limited to the results of the IQ (Intelligence Quotient) test. There has been much criticism of confining a person's intelligence to what can be measured by an IQ test. Critics do not dispute the fact that IQ tests can predict certain types of achievement rather well. But, they argue, to base our entire concept of human intelligence on IQ scores alone is to ignore many other important aspects of our abilities.[3]

In 1983, Howard Gardner suggested in his book *Frames of Mind* that people have multiple intelligences: logical, linguistic, spatial, musical, kinesthetic, intrapersonal (knowing yourself), naturalist and interpersonal (knowing others).[4] This opened educators' thinking about intelligence and some schools began to teach to these different intelligences. From there a series of expanded views of intelligence evolved.

In 1995, Daniel Goleman wrote the groundbreaking book, *Emotional Intelligence,* which sparked a new movement, one that took emotions out of the closet and put them on the forefront of awareness. Goleman's exhaustive review of the research into the nature of emotions and intelligence revealed that our success in life is based as much or more on our ability to manage our emotions than on our intellectual or analytical capabilities. He found that our ability to self-regulate and direct our emotions is critical for success in a wide range of occupations and for building and maintaining friendships.[5]

Goleman's work helped to spawn a new field of scientific inquiry called "positive psychology" based on research findings that positive emotional states actually broaden our thinking. Barbara Fredrickson's "broaden and build" theory describes how negative emotions can't get you into states that enable you to appreciate multiple points of view or facilitate problem solving and creativity. Only positive emotional states like gratitude and love can do that.[6] Now researchers are talking about a positive "collective intelligence" as human communities evolve towards higher order complexity and harmony.

When we began our research on heart intelligence, we had subjects practice heart-focused breathing techniques while generating feelings of appreciation, love, care or compassion. They frequently reported experiences of heightened intuition and insight for more effective choices in daily living. This gave us reason to suspect that heart-focused practices stimulated our intelligence beyond our normal range of perception. We understood that many sages and philosophers have talked about an intuitive intelligence that provides direct perception and clarity independent of the mind's reasoning processes. We wanted to understand the physiological pathways, so our next step was to look at how the heart and brain communicate.

Heart-Brain Research

In-depth research into the physiology of heart-brain communication began in the second half of the 20th century. During the 1960s and '70s, pioneer physiologists John and Beatrice Lacey conducted research that showed the heart actually communicates with the brain in ways that greatly affect how we perceive and react to the world around us.[7, 8]

In 1991, the year that the HeartMath Institute was established, pioneer neuro-cardiologist Dr. J. Andrew Armour introduced the term "heart brain."[9] He found that the heart possessed its own complex intrinsic nervous system that acts as a brain and functions *independently* from the brain in the head. This "heart-brain" has been shown to sense, process and encode information internally. There is evidence that the heart's brain possesses the capacity to learn, and even has short and long-term memory, and neural plasticity. Moreover, ascending neurological signals sent from the heart to the brain continuously interact with and modify the activity in the brain's higher cognitive and emotional centers.[10] In this way, input originating in the heart is a major and consistent influence in the very processes underlying our perception, cognition and emotion. At the physical level, the heart not only possesses an innate form of intelligence, but, through its extensive communication with the brain and body, the heart is intimately involved in how we think, feel and respond to the world.[1]

Today, scientists have learned a great deal more about the heart's independent and intelligent functions, which is still not common knowledge for many people, even clinicians and other researchers. Here are some of the findings:

*The heart starts beating in the unborn fetus before the brain has been formed.

*There is constant two-way communication between the heart and brain.

*The heart sends more information to the brain than the brain sends to the heart.

*The heart sends signals to the brain which help inform our choices.

*The heart helps synchronize many systems in the body so that they can function in harmony with one another.

*The heart signals especially affect the brain centers involved in strategic thinking, reaction times and self-regulation.

Emotional Self-Regulation

In the early '90s, our research center found that negative or stressful emotions threw the nervous system out of sync, and when that happened our heart rhythms became disordered and appeared jagged on a heart rhythm monitor.[11] This placed increased stress on the physical system and negatively impacted mental functions. Positive emotions like appreciation, love, care and compassion, in contrast, were found to increase order and balance in the nervous system, and produce smooth, harmonious, sine-wave like (coherent) heart rhythms. These harmonious rhythms reduced stress but they did more: *They actually enhanced people's ability to think more clearly and to self-regulate their emotional responses.*[1]

We found that through learning how to decipher the messages we receive from our heart, we gain the keen perception needed to effectively manage our emotions in the midst of life's challenges. The more we learn to listen to and follow our heart intelligence, the more balanced and coherent our emotions become. The more emotionally intelligent people are, the more they have been schooled by the wisdom and intelligence of the heart. Without the regulating influence of the heart's intelligence, our minds easily fall prey to reactive emotions such as insecurity, anger, fear and blame, as well as other energy-draining reactions and behaviors. It became evident that emotional self-regulation supports access to our heart's intelligence. In addition, mental clarity and intuition are heightened as people learn to shift into a more coherent heart rhythm, which enables them to listen and connect more deeply to their heart's intuitive signals.[12]

Heart Intelligence and Psychology

When I was a student at the University of Chicago studying psychology, I was introduced to cognitive behavioral therapy (CBT), an evolution of psychotherapy designed to help people change their perceptions and thoughts about a situation or event, which in theory would then change their emotional state. CBT is still the most common form of therapy today and many would say the most effective because it's helped millions of people. But, like most methods, CBT works better for some than others. Our deeply held emotional beliefs can undermine our mind's rational and conceptual thinking. A focus on emotional self-awareness and nonjudgmental acceptance of our feelings is often an essential first step in releasing emotional resistance. This opens the heart so that intuitive heart intelligence can provide insight that allows a bigger picture to emerge in our perceptions and facilitate mental and emotional healing.

The ability to manage our emotions, not suppress them but enable them to transform into higher quality feelings and perceptions, is essential for the advancement of individual and collective human consciousness. If we look at history, we see how emotional mismanagement resulting in blame, hate and retribution has created endless loops of suffering on our planet. The power to transform thoughts and emotions into new perceptions is facilitated by learning to listen more deeply to our heart's intuitive guidance and wisdom. This increases the ability to choose our emotional responses instead of mechanically reacting. We can learn to recognize emotions and attitudes that drain us, then replace them with emotions and attitudes that are regenerative and provide more enlightened perspectives. Gaining this ability is one of the primary benefits of practicing tools to access the heart's intelligence.

It can be challenging to distinguish the guidance of our heart from the mental and emotional beliefs that often shape our thoughts. It's encouraging to know that the more we practice discerning the difference between our heart's guidance and our mind's persuasions, it *does* get easier to distinguish. At the start, it can seem hard and discouraging at times. Yet with practice, we can learn to recognize our heart intuition has a different quality or tone than intellectual or conceptual thoughts or emotional desires and beliefs.

You may have found, as I did years ago, that following what you thought was your heart got you into trouble. For example, you might have felt a tingling and your heart beating fast about dating a certain person, but it turned out to be a bad experience. We can easily confuse an emotional sensation for our heart's intuition, and follow that allure instead. It takes practice to discern the difference. I learned through trial and error that the lure of attraction wasn't always a signal from my true heart.

The heart often whispers to us with quiet common sense. Often it's our heart telling us, "I don't know if I should take the job even though it pays a lot." Then our mind decides to take the job, because in most cases money choices usually win over heart choices until we become empowered by our higher discernment capacities. The mind tends to rationalize our desires and reactions. As my friend Amy says, *"When my mind's judgments and reactions are in control, I feel justified in being angry. My heart is decidedly different – softer and simpler. It takes courage to listen to your heart. It might say, 'Just let it go' or 'It's no big deal,' and you may be afraid you're going to let someone get away with something or that the other person is going to walk all over you. But when you have the courage to do what your heart says, you feel better and things seem to work out better."*

To help distinguish between how your head might sound versus your heart, here are some examples:

Driving at Rush Hour. *Head:* Damn this traffic! Stupid driver, slowing everyone down. When are they going to widen this road? She just cut in deliberately! *Heart:* Traffic isn't going to move until it moves—no use getting upset and draining energy. Turn on the radio and listen to some music.

At Work. *Head*: Who does she think she is? It's not fair she gets the good assignments and I'm left with crap—makes me furious! *Heart*: I know things are tough for her and she's running fast. I need to keep my cool, not get sucked into this drama and backbiting. Maybe I'm the one who needs a change in attitude. I think I'll invite her out to lunch.

As you practice listening for the difference in tone, you may find that the mind and heart are like two different radio stations. When you tune to the heart station, your attitude shifts and you look for responses that are better suited for the wholeness of the situation. The mind becomes a big winner in the process. It actually becomes more *rational*. Heart intelligence provides the mind with a bigger picture that allows it to consider what is best for oneself while being more inclusive of the wholeness.

I have also learned that the most effective way to balance my emotional nature and clear unresolved issues is to access my heart and practice self-compassion, compassion for others, appreciation and kindness. These heart-based practices have increasingly enabled me to distinguish intuitive heart feelings from mental and emotional preferences or concerns. In our research, we found that intuitive insight occurs more frequently when people are aligned with the core values of their heart. It often comes as a high-speed intuitive download activated by genuine feelings of appreciation, compassion or kindness. For example, many people talk about the benefits of appreciation or keeping a gratitude journal. We realized that when people express gratitude or appreciation, these are *acts of intelligence* that create more insight and effective outcomes (they are not just something sweet or philosophical).

Many people practice some form of prayer or meditation to discern their heart's intuitive signals. Mindfulness practice has recently become very popular. It teaches people to observe their thoughts and feelings without judging them or getting hooked into them. The practice of "loving kindness" gives you more capacity to do that and is also an important aspect of mindfulness. John Kabat-Zinn, author of numerous books on mindfulness wrote, *"Awareness, like a field of compassionate intelligence located within your own heart, takes it all in and serves as a source of peace within the turmoil, much as a mother would be a source of peace, compassion and perspective for a child who was upset. She knows that whatever is troubling her child will pass, so she can provide comfort, reassurance and peace in her very being. As we cultivate mindfulness in our own hearts, we can direct a similar compassion towards ourselves."*[13]

Humanity will in time come to realize that the heart contains a higher intelligence software package, designed to provide the intuitive guidance needed for navigating life. More people than ever are going to the heart to find greater ease and flow in life. Emotional intelligence is part of it, but people instinctively know there's something seriously intelligent about the heart or they wouldn't say, "When there is nowhere else to go for an answer, go to your heart." The fun question is, why not go there to start with, rather than everywhere else first.

In the coming chapters we will describe more of our research into our innate heart intelligence. This research has helped us understand how the heart's intelligence synthesizes other aspects of intelligence to enable us to *become who we truly are*.

*1.   McCraty, R., Atkinson, M., Tomasino, D., & Bradley, R. T, The coherent heart: Heart-brain interactions, psychophysiological coherence, and the emergence of system-wide order. Integral Review, 2009. **5**(2): p. 10-115.*

2.   Privateer, P.M., Inventing intelligence: A social history of smart2008: John Wiley & Sons.

*3.   Weinberg, R.A., Intelligence and IQ: Landmark issues and great debates. American Psychologist, 1989. **44**(2): p. 98.*

4.   Gardner, H., Frames of Mind1985, New York: Basic Books.

5.   Goleman, D., Emotional Intelligence1995, New York: Bantam Books.

*6.   Fredrickson, B.L., The role of positive emotions in positive psychology. The broaden-and-build theory of positive emotions. American Psychologist, 2001. **56**(3): p. 218-226.*

7.   Lacey, B.C. and J.I. Lacey, Studies of heart rate and other bodily processes in sensorimotor behavior, in Cardiovascular Psychophysiology: Current Issues in Response Mechanisms, Biofeedback, and Methodology., P.A. Obrist, et al., Editors. 1974, Aldine: Chicago. p. 538-564.

8.   Lacey, J.I. and B.C. Lacey, *Two-way communication between the heart and the brain: Significance of time within the cardiac cycle. American Psychologist, 1978(February): p. 99-113.*

9.   Armour, J.A., *Anatomy and function of the intrathoracic neurons regulating the mammalian heart, in Reflex Control of the Circulation, I.H. Zucker and J.P. Gilmore, Editors. 1991, CRC Press: Boca Raton. p. 1-37.*

10.   McCraty, R. and F. Shaffer, *Heart Rate Variability: New Perspectives on Physiological Mechanisms, Assessment of Self-regulatory Capacity, and Health Risk. Glob Adv Health Med, 2015. **4**(1): p. 46-61.*

11.   McCraty, R., et al., *The effects of emotions on short-term power spectrum analysis of heart rate variability. Am J Cardiol, 1995. **76**(14): p. 1089-93.*

12.   McCraty, R., M. Atkinson, and R.T. Bradley, *Electrophysiological evidence of intuition: Part 2. A system-wide process? J Altern Complement Med, 2004. **10**(2): p. 325-36.*

13.   Kabat-Zinn, J. and T.N. Hanh, *Full catastrophe living: Using the wisdom of your body and mind to face stress, pain, and illness2009: Delta.*

CHAPTER 3

THE INTUITIVE HEART
By Rollin McCraty

Most of us have been in situations where we felt in our heart the best choice, but instead gave into our mind's fears or desires. Later, we had to backtrack and clear up the problems that resulted. In the last chapter, we described heart intelligence as the *"flow of awareness, understanding and intuition guidance we experience when the mind and emotions are brought into coherent alignment with the heart."* From my own experience and my observation of others, I realized that the lack of alignment between what our mind says and what our intuitive heart is quietly trying to tell us can be one of the biggest unrecognized sources of stress. It's like being pulled in two different directions. The Greeks viewed these contrasting aspects as being in a constant struggle for control of our inner experience. I've found that intuition doesn't have to be random, fleeting or in a constant struggle with the mind. With practice, accessing intuition can become integrated into the choices and decisions of our daily lives.

In this chapter, I will provide a brief overview of some of the scientific research that HeartMath and others have done on intuition. Before describing this exciting research, it's helpful to discuss the common ways the term intuition has been defined. The root of the word "intuition" stems from the Latin word *in-tuir*, which can be translated as "looking, regarding or knowing from within." In most dictionaries, intuition is defined as "the ability to understand or know something, without conscious reasoning." A review of the scientific perspectives on the topic of intuition describe it as "a complex set of inter-related cognitive and bodily processes, in which there is no apparent intrusion of deliberate, rational thought."[1]

Types of Intuition

Historically, most of the research on intuition has focused on the purely cognitive or mental aspects of perception, where intuition is assigned to implicit processes and implicit memory. This type of intuition is a function of the unconscious mind accessing existing information stored away within our brain that we forgot we learned or did not realize we had learned.

It is generally well accepted in scientific circles that there are two separate processing systems used by the brain—this is commonly called dual-process theory. The first is unconscious, automatic and intuitive. It processes information very rapidly, looking for any similarities between what we are currently seeing or hearing then trying to find a match with past unconscious memories. Therefore, it is relatively undemanding in its use of mental resources.[1] I remember as a child spending time with my grandfather, the town mechanic, and being amazed at his ability to "just listen" to a car or truck idling and often instantly know what the problem was. When someone has gained experience in a particular field, these implicit intuitions are possible because of the brain's capacity to rapidly and unconsciously recognize important cues and match them to familiar ones. In contrast, the second processing system used by our brain is relatively slow and analytical. It's the system where we become conscious of our thoughts about a situation or issue.

Implicit processes can also explain in part what in scientific circles is often called "insight." When we encounter a new problem, one that we cannot quickly solve and may eventually put on the shelf for a while, our brain can still be working on it subconsciously. For instance, when we're in the shower, driving or doing something else unrelated to the problem, a solution pops into our conscious mind as an intuitive insight—an "aha" or "Eureka" moment. Although implicit processes are an important and common type of intuition, some scientists believe they are the only aspect of intuition. New findings are suggesting this is not the case.

In addition to the implicit memory aspect of intuition, there are two other types of sensitivities that tend to get lumped together under the term intuition which can make it confusing for people, especially as we talk about a deeper intuition that connects us with the wisdom and guidance from a higher dimensional aspect of ourselves. All three types of intuition are shown in Figure 1: implicit memory that I described above, along with a second aspect called "energetic sensitivity" and a third called "nonlocal intuition".[2]

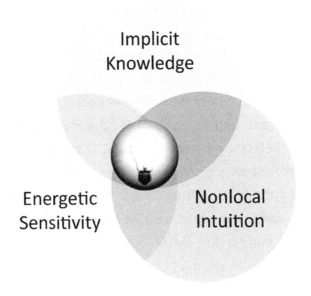

Figure 1 – Three types of sensitivities that the term intuition is used to describe.

Energetic Sensitivity

Energetic sensitivity refers to the ability of our body and nervous system to detect electromagnetic and other types of energetic signals in the environment.[3] This line of research began in our laboratory back in the early 1990s when we were doing research on water. We discovered that water had an unexpected "amplification effect" on weak electromagnetic signals. We also found that different sources of water had slightly different capacities to amplify weak signals. Knowing that the heart radiates a magnetic field which can be detected several feet outside the body with sensitive magnetometers, Mike Atkinson, our laboratory manager, and I came up with the idea to see if we could detect a person's heartbeat in a glass of water. We placed an electrode in a glass of water and then placed the glass in front of but not touching the person's chest. The experiment worked! Realizing that the human body is 80% water, our next step was obvious. We wanted to see if a person's heartbeat could be detected in another person's body and brain. Indeed, we found that we could detect this, which then led to a series of experiments that confirmed that the electromagnetic signal the heart radiates outwardly into the environment can be detected by other people and animals who are nearby. Some fun examples were described in Chapter 1 (Josh and his dog, Mabel; Ellen and her horse, Tonopah).

In the next phase of our research we were able to show that information related to our emotional state is encoded in the magnetic field radiated by the heart. In essence, what this means is that a subtle yet influential electromagnetic or "energetic" communication system operates just below our conscious awareness. This communication system energetically connects us to others and helps explain how we can feel or sense another person's presence or their emotional state, before having any cues from their body language or tone of voice.[3]

Yet another example of this type of intuition is people who are sensitive to changes in the earth's magnetic fields, many of whom experience more anxiety, increased fatigue or mental confusion during solar or magnetic storms. In fact, the data from our research suggests that we are all affected to varying degrees by the changing rhythms in the earth's magnetic fields.[4]

Nonlocal Intuition

One of the most frequent comments I have heard over the years from people who have been practicing HeartMath techniques for a while is that their intuition has noticeably increased. They also report experiencing an increased number of synchronicities. The many stories they have told me are clear examples of a type of intuition that could not be explained by past or forgotten knowledge (implicit processes) or by sensing environmental signals (energetic sensitivity). We are calling this type of intuition "nonlocal intuition" because it transcends the usual limits of time and space. A common story of nonlocal intuition I hear from people, one that you may have experienced yourself, is they spontaneously remember or start thinking about a friend from the past whom they have not talked with or thought about in a long time. Shortly after thinking about that person, the phone rings and sure enough that person is the one calling. Other common examples of nonlocal intuition are when someone has a clear sense about an event before it occurs, or a mother senses that her child in another part of the world or across town is in distress or has been injured. I have had the privilege to work with a number of law enforcement agencies over the past few years, and when I present our research on nonlocal intuition, there is almost always a story that one of the officers tells about how this type of intuition saved someone's life.

A few years ago when Dean Radin, Ph.D. the senior scientist at the Institute of Noetic Sciences, was visiting our research lab he told us about the results of a study he had recently conducted which showed that participants' autonomic nervous systems responded before they saw randomly selected photos that elicited either a negative or a calming emotional response.[5] We immediately saw that his protocol provided a rigorous tool we could use to investigate at least some aspects of nonlocal intuition.

In the following months, we expanded on his experiment by adding additional measures to determine when and where intuitive information about a future event was registering in the body and how it flowed through the body, brain and nervous system. Dr. Radin had focused on using skin conductance levels, which respond to changes in the sympathetic branch of the nervous system, as his measure of autonomic nervous system activity. In our first study, in addition to skin conductance levels (SCL), we included measures of each participant's brain waves (EEG), their heart's electrical activity (ECG), and their heart rate variability (HRV).[6, 7]

In the first of a series of studies, 26 adults who had experience using HeartMath techniques to sustain a heart coherent state completed the study procedures two different times about two weeks apart. Half of the participants completed the procedures after they had first been in a heart coherent state for 10 minutes by using a HeartMath technique called Heart Lock-In® while the other half of the participants completed the procedures without doing a Heart Lock-In. The order for both groups was then reversed for the second round of measurements so we could see if being in a coherent state was related to any differences in the results. We suspected this would be likely, as other studies we had conducted found that being in heart coherence before engaging in tasks improved performance and the ability to sustain focus.[8]

The participants thought they were participating in a study to test their stress reactions to different types of photographs, and were unaware of the study's true purpose. Each was seated in front of a computer screen and instructed to click the mouse when ready to begin each trial. After clicking the mouse, the computer screen remained blank for six seconds. At this point, after all their physiological data had been recorded, a special software program randomly selected the type of photograph to display—one that evoked either a strong emotional reaction or a calm state. The selected photo was displayed on the screen for three seconds (see Figure 2). A blank screen was then shown for an additional 10 seconds, after which a message appeared on the monitor instructing participants to click the mouse again to start the next trial when they were ready. Each participant saw 45 pictures during each of the two times they participated in the experiment. Out of the 45 pictures, 30 were known through previous research to evoke a calm response and 15 pictures were ones known to elicit a strong emotional response.

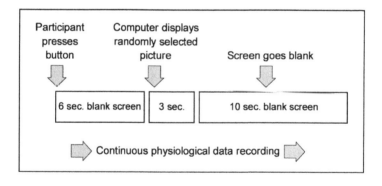

Figure 2 - Experimental setup for the study of nonlocal intuitive perception. Participants viewed a computer monitor and were instructed to press a button when ready to begin each trial. Following the button press, the screen remained blank for 6 seconds, after which the computer presented a randomly selected image from one of the two picture sets (calm or emotional) and displayed it for 3 seconds. A blank screen followed for 10 seconds. After this cool-down period, a message appeared on the monitor instructing participants to begin the next trial when ready. Intuitive (pre-stimulus) responses in this study were measured during the 6-second blank-screen period *before* the research participant viewed the randomly selected emotional or calm picture.

The study's results provided some intriguing findings and were published in two research papers as there was too much data to fit into one paper. I will provide some of the highlights here. The study showed that both the heart and the brain appeared to be receiving and responding to information about the emotional quality of the picture before the computer had randomly selected it. In other words, the heart and brain appeared to be responding to a future event before it happened—in fact 4.8 seconds before the picture was randomly selected by the computer.[6, 7] Keep in mind, the physiological data was collected before the computer had randomly selected the picture that it would display.

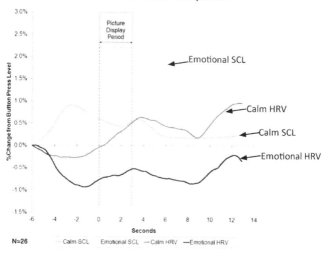

The Heart's Pre-stimulus Response

Figure 3 - The heart's pre-stimulus response. The graph shows group averages of the heart rate variability and skin conductance level responses. The "0" time point denotes when the photos were first shown, when participants saw either an emotionally arousing or calm picture. Pre-stimulus responses which indicate nonlocal intuition are in the period between −6 and 0 seconds. The highly significant difference between the HRV responses in the pre-stimulus period before the future calm or emotional photos can clearly be seen starting to diverge approximately 4.8 seconds prior to the participants actually seeing the photos. Surprisingly, there was not a significant difference in the pre-stimulus period for the skin conductance measures.

54

Even more profound was that the data showed the heart was receiving this information before the brain received it. Due to the fact that we had recorded both the brain waves and the electrocardiogram, we were able to do further analysis called heartbeat-evoked potential analysis. In essence, this allowed us to track the flow or path of the neural signals from the heart to the different regions in the brain. The important finding from this analysis showed that, depending on the emotional quality of the future picture, the heart sent a different pattern of neural signals to the brain before there was a pre-stimulus response anywhere in the brain. Shortly after the signals from the heart arrived at the brain's frontal cortex, a clear pattern of pre-stimulus signals showed up in the brain.

The analysis also found that when participants were in a heart coherent state before starting the experiment, the signals sent from the heart had a much stronger effect on changing the activity at the frontal areas of the brain. This indicates that when participants were in a more coherent state prior to the experiment, they were more attuned to the intuitive information from the heart. The results clearly suggest that the heart and brain are connected to a source of information that operates outside the classical boundaries of time and space. In physics this is called nonlocal information. These experiments also suggest that as we practice being in a more heart coherent state, we have a closer alignment to that source of information.

Further interesting results were obtained in a subsequent study conducted in Iran on nonlocal intuition that used repeat entrepreneurs as the participants. This study applied the same procedures we used in our studies (calm and emotional pictures) but they added an important twist. First they did the experiment with a group 15 participants who confirmed the results of our original study. Then they did a second experiment with 30 people, but who were in *pairs* and participating in the same procedures at the same time. This was done in order to determine if the nonlocal intuitive effect could be "amplified" by social connection. They found a significantly larger pre-stimulus effect within the pairs of participants than was found in the single participant results. The study authors stated that, *"...especially changes in the heart rhythm can detect intuitive foreknowledge. This result is notable because it constitutes cross-cultural corroboration. In addition, the results for co-participant pairs offer new evidence on the amplification of the nonlocal intuition signal."*[9]

These studies, along with others, have provided compelling evidence that nonlocal intuition can be consistently demonstrated in rigorous experimental conditions by multiple investigators.[10, 11] Furthermore, they have repeatedly demonstrated that the heart's activity appears to be the best[12] physiological indicator of nonlocal information. Somehow, information that is outside of our normal ways of thinking about time and space is available to us. Several scientific theories have been developed in an attempt to better understand how accessing this information is possible, however, no one yet really knows the specific mechanisms of how connecting with nonlocal information works.

As mentioned earlier, many perspectives and teachings over the centuries from diverse cultures around the world spoke of the heart as an access point to the wisdom of our soul or a higher source. Although we cannot say that the nonlocal intuition research described above proves that we have a soul or that there is a universal source of intelligence, it does indicate that the heart is indeed connected to a source of intelligence not bound by the limits of time and space. It just may be that science is on the verge of confirming that the majority of the historical icons of the world's spiritual traditions have been right all along.

Our theory is that there is a connection between the physical heart and the energetic or spiritual heart that provides an access point for intuitive guidance that's much more expansive and inclusive than implicit processes. In our laboratory, we use the term energetic systems to refer to the functions we cannot directly measure, touch or see, such as our emotions, thoughts and intuitions. Although these functions have clear correlations with biological activity patterns, they nevertheless remain hidden from direct measurement and observation. Several notable scientists have proposed that such functions operate primarily in the frequency domain (energetic interactions), which by definition, lies outside time and space.[12-15]

In short, our research and personal experience support the hypothesis that the energetic heart has communication channels connecting it with the physical heart, which then communicates intuitive information to the brain's emotional centers and frontal cortex. In the next chapter I will discuss how the signals from our heart can modulate our perceptions and emotional experience.

The practice of building our intuitive connection to our higher capacities is transformational. It enables us to access a source of higher information that streams into our brain and mind via our energetic heart to inform our moment-to-moment perceptions. It provides what we call practical intuition where we are more conscious and intuitive at choice points and thus get to choose our actions and reactions rather than mechanically respond in the same old stress-producing behavior patterns. We see this as the most important function of intuition.

Practical Intuition

Learning how to generate a heart coherent state to access intuitive intelligence can help prevent many stress-producing scenarios and create a much easier transit and flow through our daily challenges. Practicing heart coherence a few minutes several times a day helps to attune our mental and emotional nature to the most reasonable and effective way for responding to each situation that life brings us—challenging, normal or creative. Intuition is the voice of "who you really are."

Here are some practical situations where practicing heart coherence to access intuition can be very helpful.

- Making better choices for higher outcomes

- Increasing your capacity for discerning direction in sensitive situations

- Deciding when it's time to speak up or when it's time to hold back

- Determining what attitude you should bring to a particular situation

- Detecting when life is telling you that you need to change an attitude, disposition, etc.

- Helping guide your diet and health choices

Accessing your intuition is not one quick trick. Some think it is and that's why many people get frustrated with intuition. You have to practice opening and connecting with the heart for intuition to grow within you. Below is the simple Heart Lock-In® Technique used in the intuition study to generate a heart coherent state, which you can practice to build your intuitive connection. Opening your heart, practicing more heart connection with people and listening from the heart draws in more intuition. Self-compassion, self-forgiveness and having compassion, forgiveness and appreciation for others draws in intuition. The heart's intuition includes care for the wholeness of a situation.

Heart Lock-In® Technique

Step 1. Focus your attention in the area of the heart. Imagine your breath is flowing in and out of your heart or chest area, breathing a little slower and deeper than usual.

Step 2. Activate and sustain a regenerative feeling such as appreciation, care or compassion.

Step 3. Radiate that renewing feeling to yourself and others.

It has been my experience that accessing my intuition takes managing my emotional energy and learning to pay more attention to my heart's promptings. Otherwise, the mind and emotions tend to override the heart's often subtle promptings. As we learn to attune to our heart feelings, our natural intuitive connection can develop and grow. One of the biggest benefits of learning to follow my heart's promptings has been the ability to bring my mental and emotional faculties into greater alignment with my true self.

1.   Hodgkinson, G.P., J. Langan-Fox, and E. Sadler-Smith, Intuition: A fundamental bridging construct in the behavioural sciences. British Journal of Psychology, 2008. **99**(1): p. 1-27.

2.   McCraty, R. and M. Zayas, Intuitive Intelligence, Self-regulation, and Lifting Consciousness. Glob Adv Health Med, 2014. **3**(2): p. 56-65.

3.   McCraty, R., The Energetic Heart: Biomagnetic Communication Within and Between People, in Bioelectromagnetic and Subtle Energy Medicine, Second Edition, P.J. Rosch, Editor 2015.

4.   McCraty, R. and A. Deyhle, The Global Coherence Initative: Investigating the Dynamic Relationship between People and Earth's Energetic Systems in Bioelectromagnetic and Subtle Energy Medicine, Second Edition, P.J. Rosch, Editor 2015.

5.   Radin, D.I., Unconscious perception of future emotions: An experiment in presentiment. Journal of Scientific Exploration, 1997. **11**(2): p. 163-180.

6.   McCraty, R., M. Atkinson, and R.T. Bradley, Electrophysiological evidence of intuition: Part 2. A system-wide process? J Altern Complement Med, 2004. **10**(2): p. 325-36.

7.   McCraty, R., M. Atkinson, and R.T. Bradley, *Electrophysiological evidence of intuition: part 1. The surprising role of the heart. J Altern Complement Med, 2004.* **10**(1): p. 133-43.

8.   McCraty, R., Atkinson, M., Tomasino, D., & Bradley, R. T, *The coherent heart: Heart-brain interactions, psychophysiological coherence, and the emergence of system-wide order. Integral Review, 2009.* **5**(2): p. 10-115.

9.   Rezaei, S., M. Mirzaei, and M. Reza Zali, *Non-local Intuition: Replication and Paired-subjects Enhancement Effects. Global Advances in Health and Medicne, 2014.* **3**(2): p. 5-15.

10.   Bem, D.J., *Feeling the future: Experimental evidence for anomalous retroactive influences on cognition and affect. J Pers Soc Psychol, 2011.*

11.   Mossbridge, J., P. Tressoldi, E, and J. Utts *Predictive Physiological Anticipation Preceding Seemingly Unpredictable Stimuli: A Meta-Analysis. Frontiers in Psychology, 2012.* **3:390**.

12.   Laszlo, E., *Quantum Shift in the Global Brain: how the new scientific reality can change us and our world2008, Rochester, VT: Inner Traditions.*

13.   Mitchell, E., Quantum holography: a basis for the interface between mind and matter, in Bioelectromagnetic Medicine, P.G. Rosch and M.S. Markov, Editors. 2004, Dekker: New York, NY. p. 153-158.

14.   Pribram, K.H., Brain and Perception: Holonomy and Structure in Figural Processing1991, Hillsdale, NJ: Lawrence Erlbaum Associates, Publishers.

15.   Tiller, W.A., J. W E Dibble, and M.J. Kohane, Conscious Acts of Creation: The Emergence of a New Physics2001, Walnut Creek, CA: Pavior Publishing. (pp. 201-202).

CHAPTER 4

HEART COHERENCE: ACCESS TO HEART INTELLIGENCE

By Rollin McCraty

Many people know what it feels like to be in a state of harmony, where heart and mind are working in sync and we feel a genuine connection with others. It's easy to love this experience of inner harmony, but often times it happens by chance, rather than by design or intention. Wouldn't it be nice to be able to produce this alignment on demand, in day-to-day communications, projects and challenges?

So what empowers our ability to create more balance and harmony in ourselves, our relationships, our work and in how we handle our challenges? Through twenty years of applied research at the HeartMath Institute, we have identified a *core element,* a physiological state we call *"heart coherence"* that supports a balanced partnership in the interactions between our heart, mind, emotions and physiology. Heart coherence has been shown in numerous studies to enhance health, wellbeing, relationships and performance, in a broad range of contexts.

To help de-mystify the term *"coherence"*, let's use a simple analogy. Imagine being in meditation or prayer and being constantly interrupted by intruding thoughts, feelings, worries, mind loops or even good ideas, all of which can disrupt and scatter the focus and effectiveness of our intentions. This creates a type of internal *"incoherence"* or internal "noise." On the other hand, increasing our internal *coherence* during prayer or meditation helps us sustain and maintain a genuine, heartfelt focus which translates into increased intuitive guidance and personal effectiveness. Getting into this state of coherence helps to align and coordinate our thoughts and emotions with our heart's intelligence, so that mixed agendas or mixed signals don't scramble our minds. Incoherence is like static on a radio station we are listening to, whereas internal coherence better "tunes us in" to the station and we get a much clearer signal.

A common dictionary definition of coherence is, "the quality of being logically integrated, consistent and intelligible," as in a coherent statement. Another definition is, "the orderly and harmonious relationships among the various parts of something, whether a living system such as a human being or the cosmos." The term coherence always implies connectedness, correlation, stability and efficient energy utilization. In our physiology, a type of coherence occurs when two or more of our body's rhythmic systems, such as our breathing rhythms and heart rhythms, become synchronized at the same frequency. This is known as *physiological coherence*, a term our research center introduced to describe the degree of order, harmony and stability in the various rhythmic activities within the body's systems over any given time period. If the term coherence still seems difficult to understand, you might think of it as resonance, being in sync or in alignment.

In complex systems, such as human beings, there is a significant amount of physiological activity that has to work together in a harmonious, coordinated and synchronized manner. There are many internal systems, such as DNA, enzymes, cells, organs and glands each operating seemingly independently, doing different things at different times, yet all working together in a coordinated and synchronized dance. If this were not the case, it would be a free-for-all among the body's systems, rather than a harmoniously coordinated federation of the body's various functions. In fact, this type of "coherence" has been proposed as the quality that makes life possible.[1]

Several neuroscientists have suggested that it is the degree of harmony, resonance and *coherence* in our body's internal processes that underlies the quality and stability of the feelings and emotions we experience. The feelings we experience as "positive" reflect a coherent system, whose efficient function is directly related to the ease and flow in its processes. On the other hand, an erratic, discordant pattern of activity in the brain and nervous system denotes an incoherent system whose function reflects stress in life processes. We tend to experience this incoherent activity as unsettling or troubling feelings, such as instability, frustration, anxiety, overwhelm, impatience and so on.[2]

Not only is the term coherence used to describe harmony in our body's processes, mental and emotional ease and flow, and the efficiency and effectiveness of our words and actions, coherence also applies to social settings. *Social coherence* is reflected as a stable, harmonious alignment of relationships in a group (family, team, network, organization, etc.) which allows for the efficient flow and utilization of energy and good communication, all of which are necessary for optimal group cohesion and aligned action. When alignment occurs there is coherence between parts, and our intended results are more likely to be achieved. When relations in a group are discordant and social organization is incoherent, not only is optimal action not possible, but dysfunction and instability are likely consequences. At HeartMath, we have studied personal and social coherence in great detail, as well as how *heart coherence* facilitates the mechanics of personal and social coherence at a physiological level. Here's a simple scientific overview.

Heart Coherence

Physiological *coherence* refers to a specific state that reflects increased harmony and stability in higher-level control systems in the brain; increased synchronization between heart and brain and in the activity occurring in the two branches of the autonomic nervous system (ANS); and a general shift in autonomic balance towards increased parasympathetic activity (also known as vagal tone or activity). This physiological state, also referred to as *heart coherence* because the heart is a key instigator of this state, is associated with increased emotional balance, stability, access to intuition, and improved mental functions (ability to focus, memory, reaction times, coordination, etc.).

As mentioned in Chapter 2, research has also revealed that the physical heart has its own nervous system. Neuro-cardiologists call it the intrinsic cardiac nervous system and nicknamed it the "heart-brain".[3] The research on the structure and functions of this heart-brain has significantly benefited HeartMath research because it provides the anatomical details of how the heart and brain are in constant communication, and helps explain studies that demonstrated how the activity of the heart influences brain centers involved in our perceptions, cognitive performance and emotional experience.[4-7] An important analytical tool that provides us and other researchers with a window into the communication occurring between the heart and brain and the activity occurring in the ANS is called heart rate variability analysis.

Heart Rate Variability

Heart coherence can be measured using Heart Rate Variability analysis. Let me explain how this works. We all know that heart rate refers to how many times the heart beats in a minute and is measured in beats per minute (BPM). Heart Rate Variability (HRV) refers to the naturally occurring variations in the time between each and every pair of heartbeats (see Figure 1). It is this beat-to-beat variation that creates the heart's rhythms and when we look more closely, we can see repeating patterns in the heart's rhythms. Much of this naturally occurring variability is created because our heart and brain are communicating with each other through the autonomic nervous system. This variability occurs all the time, even when we are sleeping or resting.

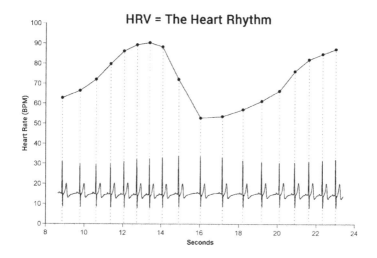

Figure 1 - This graph shows an example of the beat-to-beat changes occurring over a 24-second period. The trace on the bottom is the ECG and the dots on the top line are the instantaneous heart rate. The line that connects the dots forms the heart rhythm pattern. The upslope in the line represents an increase in heart rate, meaning there is a series of heartbeats that are speeding up (less time between heartbeats) while the downslope represents a decrease in heart rate, meaning there is a series of heartbeats slowing down (more time between heartbeats).

It was once thought that a healthy physiological state was reflected by a steady heart rhythm, where the time between each heartbeat is the same. We now know that the opposite is true! A good amount of variability is a marker of good health. In fact, many studies found that having an optimal level of variability is related to our ability to be flexible and adaptable to changing social situations and to life's challenges, both big and small.[7, 9, 10] The amount of HRV we have is even considered a measure of our health, resilience and well-being.

The amount of HRV we have over a 24 hour period is related to age, with younger people having higher levels than those who are older.[11] For someone in their twenties the heart rate will typically vary around 20 beats per minute (BPM), while someone in their seventies would tend to have a natural variability of less than 10 BPM. You can see in the bottom graph in figure 2 that the heart rate is varying from around 60 BPM to around 80 BPM, but the average heart rate is around 70 BPM. Having a lower range or amount of HRV than is normal for your age is a predictor of future health problems and is associated with numerous medical conditions.

It's well known that our perceptions and emotions can cause changes in the activity of our nervous system that can affect our heart, such as when something startles us and we feel our heart rate increase. But it's not commonly known that the signals the heart sends to the brain flow all the way into the higher centers of the brain and can have a profound influence on our higher level mental functions. For example, the heart's signals affect the activity in the cortex, that part of the brain that governs thinking and reasoning capacities. You can think of HRV as a type of complex Morse code that the heart uses to communicate with the brain and

Heart Rhythms (Heart Rate Variability)

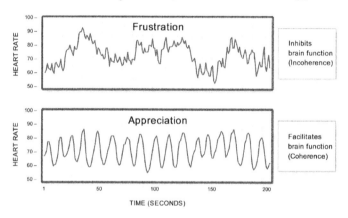

body.

Figure 2 -The two heart rhythm recordings shown in this figure are from the same person taken just moments apart. Emotions such as frustration, impatience or anxiety are reflected in an incoherent heart rhythm pattern (top). The bottom, coherent, heart rhythm pattern quickly emerged when the person used HeartMath's Quick Coherence Technique and activated a feeling of appreciation. In general, any renewing emotion such as gratitude, care, compassion or kindness tends to create more coherent heart rhythms.

In our lab during the early 1990s we conducted research on the bodily activity patterns associated with various emotional states. We measured people's hormones, immune system markers, brain waves, skin conductance, muscle activity and of course the electrocardiogram (ECG).[12-15] At that time there were very few scientific publications on positive emotions. It was through a lot of trial and error and some willing study participants, along with Doc's encouragement to have people focus on the heart and evoke warm-hearted positive feelings, like appreciation and compassion, that we observed how emotions, positive or negative, were reflected in the *patterns* of the heart's rhythm. We were able to publish this finding in *The American Journal of Cardiology*, and as far as we know, this was the first time that emotional states were linked to HRV patterns.[16]

Another important observation was that changes in the heart's rhythmic pattern were independent of heart rate (how many times a minute your heart beats). In fact, we can have a coherent or incoherent HRV pattern at a high or low heart rate. In other words, *it is the pattern or rhythm of our changing beat-to-beat heart rate, rather than heart rate itself, that is reflective of our emotional state and of how harmoniously our internal systems, including our brain, are operating.* This means that from a physiological perspective, a heart coherent state is fundamentally different than a state of relaxation, which requires only a lowered heart rate and not necessarily a coherent rhythm.

When our HRV is in a heart coherent pattern, it reflects increased *synchronization and harmony in our higher-level brain centers* and in the activity occurring in the two branches of the autonomic nervous system.

When our HRV pattern is jagged and disordered, as in the top graph of Figure 2, it's called an incoherent waveform. We found that when people were feeling sincere regenerative emotions such as love, appreciation and compassion, their heart rhythm pattern naturally became more coherent. On the other hand when they were experiencing stressful emotions such as anxiety, anger, fear or worry, a disordered, incoherent heart rhythm pattern was generated.[6]

A smooth sine-wave like HRV pattern as seen on the bottom graph of Figure 2 is called a coherent wave form. More technically speaking, physiological coherence (also referred to as heart coherence, cardiac coherence or resonance) is when the HRV pattern becomes more sine-wave like and is oscillating at a frequency of around 0.1 Hz (a 10-second rhythm), which is the natural resonant frequency of the communication system between the heart and brain.

Benefits of Coherence

Through our continued research, we found that many beneficial things happen inside the body when we are in a more coherent state. In essence, because the heart is the most powerful biological oscillator in the body, when its rhythms are "in tune" with the natural resonant frequency of the heart-brain communication system (i.e. in a state of coherence), the amplitude or amount of HRV becomes greater. When this happens the heart rhythm can pull and shift other oscillatory systems into entrainment and synchronization with it—including our breathing rhythm and blood pressure rhythms (which also vary with each heartbeat). At the same time, the brain's rhythms, such as our alpha waves, become more synchronized to the heart. All together this results in a body-wide state of increased synchronization and resonance.[6] Just being in this heart coherent state for a couple of minutes has been found to lower mean blood pressure by an average of 10 points in people with high blood pressure.[17] At the psychological level, while in a coherent state we experience a distinct quieting of the inner "noise" generated by the normal stream of unregulated mental and emotional activity. We have a greater sense of alignment and harmony, as well as connection with our heart's intuitive feelings or inner voice.

Have you ever noticed when you are emotionally upset that you have an increased tendency to say or do something you later regret? That's because feelings like anxiety, worry and fear create a type of incoherence in the nervous system and brain, resulting in what's called "cortical inhibition" where we are not as able to perceive the future consequences that our reactions and resulting words or actions may have in creating stress, energy drain and time waste. In other words, we lose our ability of foresight as our higher mental functions are taken offline![6, 7]

A growing number of research studies have shown that we can "take charge" of how we respond moment-to-moment. We can learn to better self-regulate our thoughts and emotions, which reduces and prevents many stress-producing reactions. We can do this by learning how to intentionally shift into the state of heart coherence right *in the heat of the moment*.[10, 18, 19] This creates alignment between the heart and brain resulting in "cortical facilitation" which increases our higher order capacity for mental clarity and intuitive discernment—*heart intelligence*. Increasing our heart rhythm coherence also increases emotional flexibility and adaptability, memory and our ability to focus and concentrate.[6, 20] As we gain more skill in self-regulating our mental and emotional energy expenditures and responses, we can increase our resilience, and can relatively quickly improve our health and well-being. A simple self-regulation technique that can be used to increase heart rhythm coherence is called the Quick Coherence® Technique. Many people report how effective this one-minute heart-focused breathing and emotion shifting technique has been for them in quickly recouping from challenging situations. Try it for yourself and be your own self-scientist.

Quick Coherence® Technique

Step 1: Focus your attention in the area of the heart. Imagine your breath is flowing in and out of your heart or chest area, breathing a little slower and deeper than usual.

Suggestion: Inhale 5 seconds, exhale 5 seconds (or whatever rhythm is comfortable). Putting your attention around the heart area helps you center and get coherent.

Step 2: Make a sincere attempt to experience a regenerative feeling such as appreciation or care for someone or something in your life.

Suggestion: Try to re-experience the feeling you have for someone you love, a pet, a special place, an accomplishment, etc., or focus on a feeling of calm or ease.

Establishing a New Baseline

There is a direct neural pathway from the heart to a key brain center involved in processing emotion called the amygdala. In fact, the cells at the core of the amygdala synchronize to the heartbeat. In other words, the heart rhythm pattern is informing the amygdala with important information that helps determine our emotional state. Incoherent heart rhythms can be interpreted by the amygdala as anger, anxiety or another stressful feeling, while coherent rhythms are interpreted by the amygdala as everything is okay. However, for this process to work, the amygdala needs a baseline or reference to compare the heart's incoming signals to. For example, if you're anxious a lot, then anxiety can become a familiar pattern (baseline) and feel normal.

This is how a stress habit is created. Familiar and unproductive emotional patterns, such as quick trigger reactions, getting angry, being anxious, blaming, etc., can be re-programmed as we practice getting in a heart coherent state. This state allows for increased cellular acceptance of new and beneficial patterns instated by conscious intention. This is because of the harmonious alignment that coherence creates between the heart, mind, emotions and body.

We can learn to sustain coherence for longer periods, such as during meditations, to more quickly establish a healthier new familiarized pattern in the amygdala. This creates a new inner reference or *set-point* that replaces the old non-effective emotional pattern. *Without establishing a new baseline, it's nearly impossible to sustain a desired psychological or behavioral change.* Increasing the coherent alignment between our heart, mind and emotions strengthens our capacity to change non-effective behaviors and habits that have been holding us back from accessing our higher potentials and becoming who we really are.

Assistive Coherence Building Technology

We also found that enabling people to see HRV patterns in real-time proved to be a powerful demonstration of how emotions, such as frustration and impatience, affect the activity in our nervous system and how quickly we can shift into a coherent state once we know how. It was not long until HeartMath staff who delivered training programs in hospitals, schools and companies wanted to include a "live demo" in their programs. These live demonstrations were a hit. However, the equipment was cumbersome to use, electrodes had to be stuck on the participants' chests, and our trainers needed an extra padded suitcase to transport this rather expensive lab equipment to the venue.

It became clear that the ability to see their heart rhythm pattern before and after using a HeartMath technique to shift into a coherent state, was an "ah ha" moment for most of the participants, and it accelerated their learning and practice of the coherence techniques. So we decided to see if we could create a low cost HRV coherence feedback device that anyone could use in everyday life. To do this we also needed to develop a way to quantify or measure coherent and incoherent states. It took some time, a lot of testing and trial and error, but we were eventually able to assess different levels of coherence. This was an important step in being able to design a user-friendly coherence training device. We worked with a team of software and hardware developers to create the first ever consumer friendly HRV feedback device in 1999, which was called the Freeze-Framer (named after the Freeze Frame® Technique which we teach in our training programs). Doc guided the development of some simple, short interactive games that are controlled by the user's emotional state or level of coherence to make coherence training more fun for teenagers as well as adults. At that time we had no idea we were launching what would become a new industry. At first, we wondered if anyone would buy this new computer software and sensor. But fortunately the Freeze-Framer was quickly embraced by the biofeedback industry, many health care professionals, business executives, golfers and even teachers for their classrooms. A few years later it was renamed the emWave and a portable version was also developed. Most recently a version called the Inner Balance Trainer for iOS devices (iPhones, iPods and iPads) was developed.

This technology is now used by hundreds of thousands of people as a training tool when practicing HeartMath or other techniques to increase their heart rhythm coherence. The real-time feedback has proven to be effective for helping people sustain coherence for longer periods and increases the *carryover effect* of coherent alignment into their daily activities. Sustaining coherence facilitates the process of establishing a healthy new baseline by progressively resetting the heart's rhythms to a more coherent and resonant state.

Many people who use the technology during meditation have told me that coherence level feedback helps them to quickly access a meditative state, and signals them when they lose focus, so they can shift back into a heart coherent state. I have found that coherence feedback especially helps people learn *how* to slow their mental/emotional vibratory rate so that their internal systems can operate more in sync, and they have a stronger connection with their heart's intuitive guidance.

Coherent Heart Power

There's a big pay-off from practicing *heart coherence* for even a few minutes. As we have said, being in a coherent state has a *carryover* effect.[6] This means that by spending a few minutes in a more heart coherent state before engaging in situations that are often stressful, such as before an important meeting or a challenging conversation with a client or co-worker, we are more likely to be able to sustain our inner balance and composure.

When we sit quietly in a heart coherent state, it can at times seem like not much is going on; yet from a physiological view, a lot is going on. When you're in a coherent state, your nervous system is more aligned, your hormonal and immune systems are getting rebalanced, and your mind and emotions are connecting with more of your spirit. All of this internal realignment increases resilience throughout your system.

As we increase our personal heart coherence baseline, it also benefits our families, co-workers, friends and more. From our research, we know that heart coherence is not an idle state; it reaches out, influences and supports others in many beneficial ways and expands into social coherence. Creating a healthy heart coherence baseline, individually and collectively, can provide us with more intuitive connectivity and flow, support behavior changes we want to make and enable new solutions for our personal and societal challenges.

1.   Ho, M.-W., *The Rainbow and the Worm: The Physics of Organisms*2005, Singapore: World Scientific Publishing Co.

2.   Damasio, A., *Looking for Spinoza: Joy, Sorrow, and the Feeling Brain*2003, Orlando: Harcourt.

3.   Armour, J.A., *Potential clinical relevance of the 'little brain' on the mammalian heart.* Exp Physiol, 2008. **93**(2): p. 165-76.

4.   Velden, M. and M. Juris, *Perceptual performance as a function of intra-cycle cardiac activity.* Psychophysiology, 1975. **12**(6): p. 685-92.

5.   Lacey, J.I. and B.C. Lacey, *Two-way communication between the heart and the brain: Significance of time within the cardiac cycle.* American Psychologist, 1978(February): p. 99-113.

6.   McCraty, R., Atkinson, M., Tomasino, D., & Bradley, R. T, *The coherent heart: Heart-brain interactions, psychophysiological coherence, and the emergence of system-wide order.* Integral Review, 2009. **5**(2): p. 10-115.

7.   McCraty, R. and F. Shaffer, *Heart Rate Variability: New Perspectives on Physiological Mechanisms, Assessment of Self-regulatory Capacity, and Health Risk.* Glob Adv Health Med, 2015. **4**(1): p. 46-61.

8.   Cameron, O.G., *Visceral Sensory Neuroscience: Interception*2002, New York: Oxford University Press.

9.   Segerstrom, S.C. and L.S. Nes, Heart rate variability reflects self-regulatory strength, effort, and fatigue. Psychol Sci, 2007. *18*(3): p. 275-81.

10.   McCraty, R. and M. Zayas, Cardiac coherence, self-regulation, autonomic stability, and psychosocial well-being. Frontiers in Psychology, 2014. *5*(September): p. 1-13.

11.   Umetani, K., et al., Twenty-four hour time domain heart rate variability and heart rate: relations to age and gender over nine decades. J Am Coll Cardiol, 1998. *31*(3): p. 593-601.

12.   McCraty, R., et al., Music enhances the effect of positive emotional states on salivary IgA. Stress Medicine, 1996. *12*(3): p. 167-175.

13.   McCraty, R., M. Atkinson, and W.A. Tiller, New electrophysiological correlates associated with intentional heart focus. Subtle Energies, 1995. *4*(3): p. 251-268.

14.   McCraty, R., et al., The impact of a new emotional self-management program on stress, emotions, heart rate variability, DHEA and cortisol. Integr Physiol Behav Sci, 1998. *33*(2): p. 151-70.

15.   Tiller, W.A., R. McCraty, and M. Atkinson, Cardiac coherence: a new, noninvasive measure of autonomic nervous system order. Altern Ther Health Med, 1996. *2*(1): p. 52-65.

16.   McCraty, R., et al., The effects of emotions on short-term power spectrum analysis of heart rate variability. Am J Cardiol, 1995. *76*(14): p. 1089-93.

17.   Alabdulgader, A., Coherence: A Novel Non-pharmacological Modality for Lowering Blood Pressure in Hypertensive Patients. Global Advances in Health and Medicne, 2012. **1**(2): p. 54-62.

18.   McCraty, R. and M. Atkinson, Resilence Training Program Reduces Physiological and Psychological Stress in Police Officers. Global Advances in Health and Medicine, 2012. **1**(5): p. 44-66.

19.   Ginsberg, J.P., Berry, M.E., Powell, D.A., Cardiac Coherence and PTSD in Combat Veterans. Alternative Therapies in Health and Medicine, 2010. **16**(4): p. 52-60.

20.   Lloyd, A., Brett, D., Wesnes, K., Coherence Training Improves Cognitive Functions and Behavior In Children with ADHD. Alternative Therapies in Health and Medicine, 2010. **16**(4): p. 34-42.

CHAPTER 5

SOCIAL COHERENCE
By Howard Martin

When I was a young man in the 1970s I remember driving into Washington, D.C., from Northern Virginia. All around me were high-rise apartments that extended for miles and miles. I imagined all the people inside and wondered, like many others have, "How can so many adults and children develop a new consciousness or way of thinking needed to solve our mounting personal and social problems?" I knew that positive changes do happen for many people as they mature, often through trial and error, "the school of hard-knocks." But this growth process is too slow to meet the increasing challenges that our world is facing. As I continued to pass the forest of buildings, I also wondered, "What if the positive changes each person makes contribute to an overall field of consciousness that we all draw from to co-create our reality—what if there is some way we can contribute to that field that will make it easier for others to make their own changes? Back then I didn't have a scientific understanding to verify the correctness of my feeling, but today, I have a lot to draw from.

The Energetic Field

Fast forward twenty years. It was confirming to me when HeartMath researchers discovered in 1996 that when an individual is in a state of heart rhythm coherence their heart radiates a more coherent electromagnetic signal into the environment that can be detected by the nervous systems of other people and even animals. It wasn't surprising to learn that the heart generates the strongest magnetic field in the body, approximately 100 times stronger than that produced by the brain. This field can be detected several feet from the body with sensitive magnetometers. The heart's electromagnetic field provides a plausible mechanism for how we can "feel" or sense another person's presence and emotional state independent of body language or other factors.[1]

What I found even more validating was a later study that examined whether people trained in heart coherence could energetically facilitate coherence in other people who were in close proximity but not touching. This study found that the heart coherence of an untrained participant was indeed facilitated by others who were in a coherent state. It also provided evidence of heart rhythm synchronization between people or social coherence.[2] Here's a brief summary:

There were forty participants and ten card tables with four subjects placed around each card table. Three were trained in HeartMath coherence techniques and the fourth was not. All four were hooked up to equipment that measured their heart rhythms. The three HeartMath trained participants were instructed to practice the Heart Lock-In Technique to increase their coherence and silently radiate/send positive feelings to the untrained participant who was instructed to just sit quietly. When the three HeartMath trained participants reached a sustained level of high coherence, the fourth person went into a higher state of coherence. It was as though the untrained subject had become energetically lifted into heart coherence. In addition, there a statistical relationship between this synchronization and a feeling of emotional bonding among the participants. The authors of the study concluded that, "evidence of heart-to-heart synchronization across subjects was found which lends credence to the possibility of heart-to-heart bio-communications."

A More Coherent Society

In social science terminology, *social coherence* is reflected as a stable, harmonious alignment of relationships that allows for the efficient flow of energy and communication. Social coherence can expand to a family, group or organization in which a network of relationships exists among individuals. Social coherence requires that group members be attuned and emotionally aligned and that the group's energy is regulated by care, not by threat or force from others. For example, in a coherent team, there is freedom for individual members to do their part and thrive while maintaining cohesion and resonance within the group's intent and goals.[3]

Many researchers are interested these days in understanding energetic social dynamics. Sociologist Raymond Bradley in collaboration with neuroscientist Karl Pribram developed a general theory of social communication to explain the patterns of social organization common to most groups. Bradley and Pribram found that most high functioning groups have a global organization and coherent network of emotional energetic relations interconnecting virtually all members. They found that positive energy is required to shift a system into a more coherent mode, and the key to creating stable, coherent groups is related to increasing positive emotions and dissipating negative emotional tensions, interpersonal conflicts, and other stressors within and among the individuals in that group.[4]

A growing body of evidence suggests that an energetic field can form between individuals in a group through which communication among all the group members occurs. In other words, there is a literal group "field" that connects all the members. As more individuals within a group (sports team, workplace, school classroom, social group, etc.) increase their heart coherence, the group increases in social coherence and can achieve its objectives more harmoniously and effectively.[3]

In their paper *Social Baseline Theory: The Role of Social Proximity in Emotion and Economy of Action,* Drs. Lane Beckles and James A. Coan from University of Virginia, documented the benefits of emotionally-connected interactions between people.[5] I found one aspect of their work particularly fascinating with regard to the energetic influence we can have on one another's perceptions. They wrote:

"The brain modifies sensory perception in ways that bias decision-making to manage energy use efficiently.[6] For example, wearing a heavy backpack makes distances seem further away and uphill inclines seem steeper.[7] In recent work by Schnall, Harber, Stefanucci, & Proffitt, hill slants were judged as less steep when participants stood next to a friend.[8] Moreover, this effect was moderated by the duration of the friendship— the longer the friendship, the less steep the hill."

In essence what they are describing is that our perception of walking uphill is different when we are in emotional resonance with someone. The deeper the emotional connection, the less steep the hill appears. I have found this true in my life. Most weekends I hike with a group of friends in the Santa Cruz Mountains. The hills seem much higher and hiking a lot harder when I'm by myself. What I take from this is that life gets easier and we can better achieve our goals as we develop heart-based relationships.

What about negative social coherence some may ask. Isn't there a lot of emotional resonance within fanatical groups or movements that seek to dominate or impose their beliefs on others? When a group's emotional bonding is motivated by the desire to inflict mental, emotional or physical harm on others, they are resonating in a lower vibrational intention that doesn't include the heart's discernment. The heart's intelligence by its very nature is inclusive, and heart coherence activates higher centers of the brain that experience compassion and the desire to help others develop their higher potentials. Social coherence enables a "collective intelligence" that helps raise the vibratory rate of the individuals and the group's energetic field.

MIT Sloan School of Management professor Dr. C. Otto Scharmer describes "collective intelligence" as going from ego-system to eco-system as groups evolve towards a higher order harmony and quality. He offers "U Theory" as the capacity for people to work together with "Open Mind, Open Heart and Open Will." "U" theorists and researchers Joseph Jaworski and Jane Corbett found that this can be deepened through practice of heart-based awareness tools. Corbett wrote, *"Collective intelligence can be rapidly activated to share insights and crystallise future possibilities, even in previously stuck situations, and then take skillful action in prototyping and embedding change."[9]*

In today's society there is often a "surface level" harmony where people are basically civil and cooperative. That is of course important and has led to a global society that has order. However, in most groups, large or small, many individuals understandably have anxieties, judgments, frustrations, biases and preconceptions of each other or of other groups. These feelings, said or unsaid, are energetically communicated and create separations or "closed hearts" that result in miscommunications, relational problems, and also health problems.[3]

Social coherence is happening more and more as the planetary shift is accelerating. However, in many cases it takes a significant event for larger numbers of people to collectively open their hearts. For example, often we see an increase in social coherence after a tragedy. Events such as natural disasters tend to open people's hearts, bring people together and lead them to put aside negative attitudes to work cooperatively to benefit the community. Then as time passes and normalcy returns, the community spirit that was ignited by a dramatic event often fades, as people revert to their familiar, operational baselines. Yet, on the other hand, many people are amazed at what they were able to accomplish together and the lasting friendships and bonds they forged.

The bottom-line is this: As groups of people make efforts to increase their heart coherence, it adds to a momentum of positive, evolutionary change which is what will help society to re-shape itself.

Emergence of Social Coherence

Another indicator of more social coherence emerging can be seen in ways some large brands are shifting their marketing focus away from themselves and onto the positive contribution they can make in the world. The number of Super Bowl 2015 commercials with messages of care and heart connection was truly surprising to me. The retail department store chain, Target®, enjoyed unexpected social media exposure due to a sincere act of kindness by an employee. When a teenage boy stopped by a Target in search of a clip-on tie for a job interview, a Target team member took the time to help the nervous teen put on his new tie and showed him how to do a proper handshake and tackle a few tough interview questions. This sincere moment was caught in a video, then was shared online and quickly became a viral sensation. This simple act and the exposure it generated played perfectly into Target's tagline, *"Expect More, Pay Less, Each and Every Day at Target®."* Marketing guru Simon Mainwaring, author of *We First,* commented, *"Nothing resounds more loudly among today's media-savvy audience than an authentic act of human kindness. If there is a lesson to be gained from this [Target's] experience, it's that authentic simple acts of genuine kindness resonate as loudly, if not more loudly, than any multi-million dollar campaign."*

More and more companies are focusing on purpose-driven marketing because social purpose and better health are important to millennials and other consumers. Whatever the motives of these companies in trying to sell their products, they are increasingly recognizing that customers want to feel genuine care, connection and kindness—and that these heart-based qualities are an emerging social trend. We all stand to benefit from this unfolding awareness. Sure there's a lot more to be done but we need to appreciate the steps these companies are taking, and appreciate ourselves for the steps we're taking to upgrade our personal behaviors as well.

The Heart of Leadership

Developing a more heart-based approach to business is also becoming more popular in today's work environments, although it's certainly not a movement yet. It's slowly becoming accepted that people do better (and so does the company's balance sheet) when they work in an atmosphere of care and appreciation rather than fear and stress. More employees are feeling a sense that there's more to them, and have the urge to become *who they truly are*. They are recognizing the difference between what they've been and the new person they're trying to be, and they want to follow their heart. As Steve Jobs said in a commencement address, shortly after he was diagnosed with cancer, *"Have the courage to follow your heart and intuition. They somehow already know what you truly want to become. Everything else is secondary."*

These are extraordinary times in that there's new openness and innovation, yet many aspects of organizational structure operate in a very dysfunctional way. The effects are seen and quantified in soaring health care costs, increased absenteeism, job dissatisfaction and poor decisions. It's difficult for leaders in most organizations to see how to get from where they are to where they want to be.

Some of the immediate and practical benefits of increasing coherence in organizations that we've seen include: better emotional self-management, more authentic communication, fewer mistakes, increased energy and productivity, more creativity and intuition, better decision making and more. A work environment where people move and flow with greater equilibrium and warmth, treat each other with compassion and care and have more heart intelligence to cut through challenges in a way that's best for all concerned, is a satisfying place to spend eight or more hours a day. In today's world of high-speed change and constant connectivity, leaders and employees need to be smarter and more intuitive than before to maximize potentials. A leader with business heart is not soft, but knows that a strong heart and clear head are both essential.

James K. Clifton, chairman and chief executive officer of the Gallup Organization reported that successful organizations can learn to build sustainable growth by harnessing the power of human emotions. He says that companies have learned how to be lean and mean, but need to discover a new way to manage human nature and unlock human potential. This requires understanding human emotion.

I saw a TV interview with departing Costco® CEO James Sinegal that depicts a corporate leader's emphasis on the importance of positive emotion in business and also represents a growing change in corporate culture—one that is more heart-centric and socially coherent. Sinegal was known for his focus on making Costco a great place to work and the interview showed him visiting stores and interacting with employees at all levels in a warm and caring way. At the end of the interview he was asked if there would be changes coming to Costco after he left. He responded by saying of course there would be. He went on to say that he hoped the corporate culture he had created would be preserved, adding, *"Culture is not the most important thing in business. It is the only thing."*

HeartMath coherence training programs help people learn to generate an alignment of heart, mind and emotions, resulting in increased resilience, health, creativity and other outcomes desired by most individuals, health professionals and organizations. Heart coherence training enables individuals and teams to develop self-regulation skills and access their heart's intuitive intelligence, with almost immediate health and performance benefits. Pre- and post-assessments in organizations provide validation that increasing personal and social coherence creates a higher level of individual and collective functioning to facilitate a healthier culture. I will share meta-analysis data from a few studies to offer a picture of possibilities as more and more groups and organizations start to make a greater connection to the heart's intelligence.

#1 Five Global Companies

In a large study conducted in five different global companies in Europe and the U.S., coherence training produced some significant results. The composite data from pre- and post-psychometric survey assessments of over 5,700 individuals shown in the graphs below found that, in just six to nine weeks, practice of HeartMath coherence tools produced the following average outcomes in people who reported having these symptoms *often – always:* 44% drop in fatigue; 52% drop in anxiety; 60% drop in anger; 60% drop in depression; 33% improvement in sleep. In addition, there were similar improvements in physical health among those who reported having these symptoms *often – always:* 44% drop in body aches and pains; 43% reduction in indigestion; 63% reduction in rapid heart-beats; and 44% drop in muscle tension.

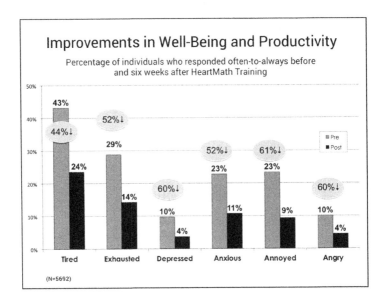

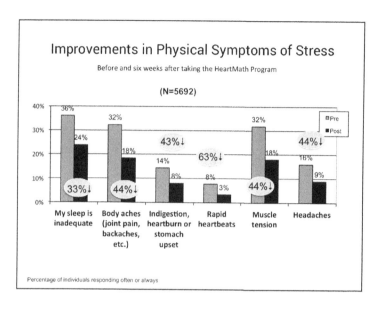

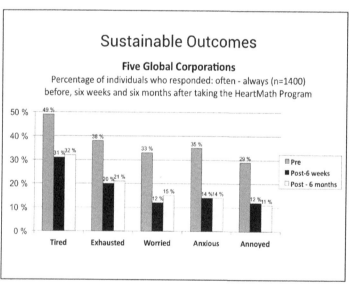

Post-assessments done again after six months and then again after one year by some of the organizations showed sustained improvements. Participants also reported significantly decrease overwhelm and intent to leave their job. What was interesting to me is that one of the company managers told us that some employees continued to practice the tools they learned while many others didn't. (That would be a typical response to any training program.) Nevertheless, improvements occurred and were sustained across the entire population. Some managers/leaders commented that something in the overall environment changed through the efforts made by only a portion of the people, which made it easier for others to achieve the positive benefits.

This intriguing finding conveys the potential of social coherence, just as we observed in the study mentioned at the start of this chapter where the heart rhythm coherence of three people facilitated an unconscious shift into heart rhythm coherence in a fourth person sitting around a table. The prospect of a social coherence multiplier effect is exciting to organizations that want to create a healthier and more caring culture.

#2 Health Care Systems

Hospitals and healthcare organizations have been early adopters of our programs, which isn't surprising since health care workers are deeply aware of the relationship between health and costs. This chart shows a meta-analysis of over 8,700 health care workers from several health care systems pre and post HeartMath training. Note the significant changes in emotional states and stress symptoms in this large population.

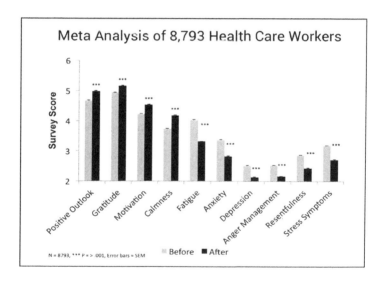

110

Many of these hospitals also measured costs savings. Several calculated they saved over $1M per year in reduced turnover and absenteeism, and determined that the program provided more than 10 times ROI (Return on Investment). As hospital leaders and staff learned HeartMath tools to transform stress and increase resilience, it also facilitated a shift to a more caring culture that permeated the hospital, increasing patient satisfaction. Here is one story.

Fairfield Medical Center (FMC) in Lancaster, Ohio, implemented HeartMath as an organization-wide initiative to improve quality of life for staff and quality of care for patients. To achieve FMC's enduring social mission: *"to be a hospital of excellence, caring for staff, patients and the community,"* this 2,000+ strong team of healthcare providers adopted the HeartMath approach *"to provide efficient, compassionate, safe, high quality healthcare for FMC patients and their families."* As of this writing, 1,120 FMC employees have been trained in HeartMath methods, nearly 54% of FMC's total workforce, and HeartMath training is now required for all new hires.

Based on three years of monitoring and evaluation, the HeartMath program at the Fairfield Medical Center delivered the following results:

* Short-term disability claims decreased 57% as compared to the previous year's claims costs.

* FMC received the Platinum Fit Friendly Company Award from the American Heart Association in 2009. In 2010, they were honored with the HeartMath Hospital designation as well as HeartMath's Continuity of Care award.

* Based on the FMC employee satisfaction survey, HeartMath trained employees reported higher job satisfaction than non-HeartMath trained staff, as well as reduced physical stress symptoms and improvements in vitality, resiliency and emotional intelligence.

Cynthia Pearsall, Chief Nursing Officer at Fairfield Medical Center and a HeartMath certified trainer describes how this works. *"When you feel stressed",* she explains *"you can literally flip the switch anytime, any-*

place, into the 'stress free zone' by changing the instant message the heart sends to the brain by way of the nervous system. I start every day with a HeartMath technique called 'Heart Lock-In' to strengthen my ability to sustain a coherent state, to achieve balance and synchronization between my heart and mind, and to become more resilient to the stresses I am sure to face throughout the day. I even begin all of my meetings this way, with a 90-second Heart Lock-in; and if we are having a difficult time reaching a decision as a team, I will ask each of us to take a couple minutes to practice some easy coherence steps to change the quality of the moment. Once the meeting resumes, we can reliably reach a decision. HeartMath is bringing this family of caregivers, indeed this local community, closer together."

Cynthia's example represents how applying the coherence building tools together helped to create a change in the hospital's culture that saved money and improved health and performance. But most importantly to her, practicing HeartMath helped her team get along better as a result of more authentic communication.

#3 Educational Outcomes

Another area where we have seen benefits from increased individual and social coherence is in educational environments. A controlled study funded by the U.S. Department of Education that involved approximately 1,000 tenth grade students practicing Heart-Math techniques along with heart coherence technology resulted in a significant *coherence baseline* increase in four months.[10] The experimental group was taught "TestEdge®," a HeartMath program to reduce test anxiety and improve academic test scores. The graph below shows the physiological changes in baseline coherence in two students that reflected the findings of the overall group before and four months after training. These coherence baseline changes correlated with improved behaviors, reduced test anxiety, and increased test scores.

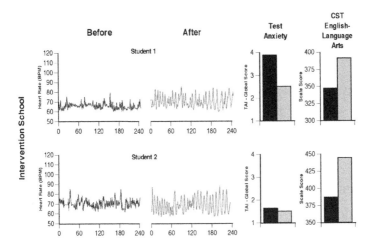

Prior to the TestEdge program, 61% of students reported being affected by test anxiety, with 26% experiencing high levels of test anxiety often or most of the time. Those with high levels of test anxiety scored, on average, 15 points lower on standardized tests in both Mathematics and English-Language Arts than students with low test anxiety. Of those students who reported being affected by test anxiety at the start of the TestEdge program, 75% had reduced levels of test anxiety by the end of the study.

The reduction in test anxiety was correlated with improvements in socio-emotional and behavioral measures in the HeartMath group: reduction in Negative Affect (feelings of stress, anger, disappointment, sadness, depression, and loneliness); reduction in Emotional Discord, reflecting increased emotional awareness and improved emotional management; and reduction in Interactional Difficulty, reflecting increased empathy and improved relations with others. In addition, there was an increase in Positive Class Experience, reflecting perception of increased enjoyment and learning in class, positive feelings toward classmates, and teacher care. Finally, there was also a significant increase in academic test scores in the HeartMath trained group over the control group, ranging on average from 10 to 25 points.

HeartMath scientific advisory board member, and a trusted mentor on many of our research studies, the late Karl Pribram, MD, Ph.D., (former Director of Stanford University's Brain Research center, author of *Brain and Perception* and *Languages of the Brain*) was most passionate about our research in education. He wrote, *"I was thrilled to read HeartMath's comprehensive report on the results of the TestEdge National Demonstration Study. The study is superb...(and) yielded an impressive body of cross-corroborating evidence docu-*

menting the effectiveness of the TestEdge program in reducing student test anxiety and improving test performance. Of particular import is the physiological evidence indicating that students in the program had established a new set point of emotional stability, a requisite for sustained behavioral change. The study is an exemplar of how social science experiments in open field research settings ought to be done."

What moved me most when I reviewed these study results was not only did test scores improve, so did social-emotional learning and positive behavioral changes. Teaching children emotional self-regulation skills and heart coherence tools will serve these young people throughout life.

Creating a Heart-Connected Society

Heart connection is on the rise because people around the world are yearning for it. They are tired of the old ways of doing things—societal systems that don't work well anymore, belief systems that focus on polarization and separation, and a host of other paradigms that have been the status quo.

It's also true that there are a tremendous amount of competing agendas in today's world, resulting in everything from serious debate to political and religious upheavals and wars. The world's problems are on full display. Yet, there is plenty of hopeful news to consider in the midst of the perceived chaos. Many people are sensing that the collective global stir is part of a shift and transition into a new consciousness based on care, cooperation and acceptance. It's the process of a new world birthing itself in the midst of the old one. Awareness is shifting, people are changing, society is transforming and a new collective intelligence is emerging.

Try for a moment to disengage from the chaos we often see in society and think about this. What if many more people came to realize the transforming potentials available within the heart of who they truly are? That what they have sensed about "heart" is real and not something only talked about in spirituality or philosophy. That by connecting with their heart's intelligent discernment, they can better manage their emotions; experience more compassion, appreciation and love; and improve their health, relationships, and performance. What if increasingly more people unleashed the power of coherent alignment and partnership between their mind, emotions and their heart's intuitive guidance for navigating their daily interactions? What kind of socially coherent world might that be? When I think about these possibilities I see a new, different and better world coming into view. From the eyes of the heart, I can see all these things coming to pass.

1.   McCraty, R., *The Energetic Heart: Biomagnetic Communication Within and Between People*, in *Bioelectromagnetic and Subtle Energy Medicine, Second Edition*, P.J. Rosch, Editor 2015.

2.   Morris, S.M., *Facilitating collective coherence: Group Effects on Heart Rate Variability Coherence and Heart Rhythm Synchronization.* Alternative Therapies in Health and Medicine, 2010. **16**(4): p. 62-72.

3.   McCraty, R., Childre, D, *Coherence: Bridging Personal, Social and Global Health.* Alternative Therapies in Health and Medicine, 2010. **16**(4): p. 10-24.

4.   Bradley, R.T. and K.H. Pribram, *Communication and stability in social collectives.* Journal of Social and Evolutionary Systems, 1998. **21**(1): p. 29-80.

5.   Beckes, L. and J.A. Coan, *Social baseline theory: The role of social proximity in emotion and economy of action.* Social and Personality Psychology Compass, 2011. **5**(12): p. 976-988.

6.   Riener, C.R., et al., *An effect of mood on the perception of geographical slant.* Cognition and Emotion, 2011. **25**(1): p. 174-182.

7.   Stefanucci, J.K., et al., *Distances appear different on hills.* Percept Psychophys, 2005. **67**(6): p. 1052-1060.

8.   Twedt, E., C.B. Hawkins, and D. Proffitt, Perspective-taking changes perceived spatial layout. Journal of Vision, 2009. *9*(8): p. 74-74.

9.   Corbett, J., In the Field and at the Heart of Presencing: Connecting Inner Transformation in Leadership with Organisational and Societal Change, in Leadership for a Healthy World: Creative Social ChangeIn press 2016.

10.   Bradley, R.T., et al., Emotion self-regulation, psychophysiological coherence, and test anxiety: results from an experiment using electrophysiological measures. Appl Psychophysiol Biofeedback, 2010. *35*(4): p. 261-83.

CHAPTER 6

GLOBAL COHERENCE
By Deborah Rozman

As I was waking up this morning and before I opened my eyes, these thoughts flooded into my consciousness: The world needs as much care and compassion as it can get. What if we could collectively put out enough pure radiant love into the earth's energetic fields that it would create a multiplier effect or a quantum coherence effect? What will it really take to shift the consciousness of humanity? These thoughts stayed with me through my morning meditation as I radiated as much pure love, care and compassion to the planet and humanity as I could.

When Sir Roger Penrose attended a conference in 1998 at the HeartMath Institute on whether quantum processes were involved in brain function, I asked him, "What is quantum coherence?" He replied, "This is when large numbers of particles can collectively cooperate in a single quantum state." I wondered if this could apply on a macro scale of people as well. Later, I read in Mae-Wan Ho's book *The Rainbow and the Worm* that quantum coherence is what defines any living system. She also wrote, *"A quantum coherent state thus maximizes both global cohesion and also local freedom! Nature presents us with a deep riddle that compels us to accommodate seemingly polar opposites..."* This riddle certainly describes the current state of our world. I pondered, "How does nature create global cohesion and also allow for free will?"

We learned in the last chapter that research findings have shown that as we practice heart coherence and radiate love and compassion, our heart generates a coherent electromagnetic wave into the local field environment that facilitates *social coherence*, whether in the home, workplace, classroom or sitting around a table. As more individuals radiate heart coherence, it builds an energetic field that makes it easier for others to connect with their heart. So, theoretically it is possible that enough people building individual and social coherence could actually contribute to an unfolding global coherence.

Science is beginning to acknowledge that we are all part of a vast web of connections that encompass not only life on this planet but the solar system and beyond. It is through this *energetic connectivity* that information, heart coherence and resonance are exchanged. Let's look at how this energetic connectivity could potentially increase global coherence.

As said before, the term "coherence" implies order, structure, harmony—an alignment within and amongst systems—whether quantum particles, organisms, human beings, social groups, planets or galaxies. This harmonious order signifies a coherent system whose optimal functioning is directly related to the ease and flow in its processes.[1]

The inner state of heart coherence is what a lot of meditation techniques (often unknowingly) attempt to achieve. There are thousands of groups and organizations all around the world using various forms of meditation or prayer to energetically help make things easier for others. Many organizations conduct synchronized meditations, prayers, intention experiments and so forth to facilitate healing or to create a more harmonious world. Numerous studies have shown that group or collective meditation, prayer and focused intention directed toward a specific positive outcome can have increased beneficial and measurable effects.

For example, a study conducted in 1993 in Washington, D.C., showed a 25% drop in crime rate when 2,500 meditators meditated during specific periods of time with that intention, which means that a relatively small group of a few thousand was able to influence a much larger group—a million and a half.[2] The question was then posed that if crime rates could be decreased, could a group of meditators also influence social conflicts and wars? A similar experiment was done during the peak of the Israel–Lebanon war in the 1980s. Drs. Charles Alexander and John Davies at Harvard University organized groups of experienced meditators in Jerusalem, Yugoslavia, and the United States to meditate and focus attention on the area at various intervals over a 27-month period. After adjusting for variant influences, such as weather changes, Lebanese, Muslim, Christian and Jewish holidays, police activity, fluctuation in group sizes, etc., during the course of the study, the levels of violence in Lebanon decreased between 40% and 80% each time a meditating group was in place, with the largest reductions occurring when the numbers of meditators were largest. During these periods, the average number of people killed during the war per day dropped from 12 to three, a decrease of more than 70%. War-related injuries fell by 68% and the intensity level of conflict decreased by 48%.[3, 4] Quantum physicist John Hagelin concluded from this research on the "Power of the Collective" that *since meditation provides an effective, scientifically proven way to dissolve individual stress and if society is composed of individuals, then it seems like common sense to use meditation to similarly diffuse societal stress.*[5]

Every individual's energy affects the collective field environment. This means each person's emotions and intentions generate an energy that affects the field. A first step in diffusing societal stress in the global field is for each of us to take personal responsibility for our own energies. We can do this by increasing our personal coherence and raising our vibratory rate, which helps us become more conscious of the thoughts, feelings and attitudes that we are "feeding the field" each day. We have a choice in every moment to "take to heart" the significance of intentionally managing our energies. This is the free will or local freedom that can create global cohesion.

Each of us is also responsible for allowing thoughts and feelings of frustration, worry or blame to run unmanaged in our system. These attitudes and emotions keep our inner rhythms incoherent and out of sync, which has a depleting *carryover* effect on our hormonal, immune and nervous systems. Heart coherence practices and technology can assist us in resetting our emotional energy and shifting into a balanced inner rhythm. They help us increase our vibratory rate and coherence baseline, so our spirit, heart, brain and nervous system operate in sync and with increased efficiency. This coherence *carryover* effect enables us to be more conscious and intuitive at choice points—to move in a state of ease and choose our actions and reactions rather than mechanically responding in the same old stress-producing patterns.

Through raising our vibratory rate, we become conscious that our energetic heart is coupled to a deeper part of our self. Many call this their "higher power" or their "higher capacities," and links us to a non-local field of information and energy that physicist David Bohm called the implicate order and undivided wholeness.[6] When we are in heart coherence, we have a tighter alignment with the heart intelligence that connects us to that source.

The Global Coherence Initiative

In 2008 the HeartMath Institute launched the Global Coherence Initiative (GCI). GCI is an international cooperative effort to help activate the heart of humanity and facilitate a shift in global consciousness. I am honored to be a member of the Global Coherence Initiative Steering Committee and to contribute to this vision. GCI has three primary focuses. The first is to invite people to participate by actively adding more heart coherent love, care and compassion into the planetary field. The second is scientific research on how we are energetically interconnected with each other and the earth; and the third is to educate people on how we can utilize this interconnectivity to more quickly raise our personal and collective vibratory rate to create a better world.

Here are a few hypotheses that guide GCI's ongoing research, in collaboration with other institutions:

The earth's magnetic fields are a carrier of biologically relevant information that connects all living systems.

1. Every person affects this global information field. Large numbers of people creating heart-coherent states of love, appreciation, care and compassion can generate a more coherent field environment that benefits others and helps off-set the current planetary discord and incoherence.

2. There is a feedback loop between human beings and the earth's energetic/magnetic systems.

3. Earth has several sources of magnetic fields that affect us all. Two of them are the geomagnetic field that emanates from the core of the earth, and the fields that exist between the earth and the ionosphere. These fields surround the entire planet and act as protective shields blocking out the harmful effects of solar radiation, cosmic rays and other forms of space weather. Without these fields, life as we know it could not exist on Earth. They are part of the dynamic ecosystem of our planet.

Scientists know a lot about these energetic fields, yet many mysteries remain. One thing that is clear is that solar activity and the rhythms taking place in the earth's magnetic fields have an impact on health and behavior.[7] A large body of research has shown that numerous physiological rhythms and global collective behaviors *are not only synchronized with solar and geomagnetic activity, but that disruptions in these fields can create adverse effects on human health and behaviors.*[8-10] When the earth's magnetic field environment is disturbed, it can cause sleep problems, mental confusion, unusual lack of energy or a feeling of being on edge or overwhelmed for no apparent reason. Sound familiar? At other times, when the earth's fields are stable and certain measures of solar activity are increased, people report increased positive feelings and more creativity and inspiration.[11] This is likely due to a coupling between the human brain, cardiovascular and nervous systems with resonating geomagnetic frequencies.

The earth and ionosphere generate a symphony of frequencies ranging from 0.01 hertz to 300 hertz. Some of these are in the exact same frequency range as those occurring in our cardiovascular system, brain and autonomic nervous system[7]. This helps explain how fluctuations in the earth's and sun's magnetic fields can affect us. Changes in the earth's fields have been shown to affect our brain waves and heart rhythms, and have been associated with changes in memory and other tasks; athletic performance; number of reported traffic violations and accidents; mortality from heart attacks and strokes; and incidence of depression and suicide.[7] Changes in the earth's fields from high solar activity have also been linked to some of humanity's greatest flourishing of creativity and art.[12] This implies the increased solar activity is not necessarily problematic; but rather it's how we respond to and manage this increased energy.

GCI scientists suggest that because we have brain wave and heart rhythm frequencies overlapping the earth's field resonances, we are not only receivers of biologically relevant information, but *we also feed information into the global field environment and essentially create a feedback loop with the earth's magnetic fields*.[11, 13] In fact, research is indicating that human emotions and consciousness *encode* information into the geomagnetic field and this encoded information is distributed globally. The earth's magnetic fields act as carrier waves for this information which influences all living systems and the collective consciousness. To further test this hypothesis and research, GCI has created a Global Coherence Monitoring System (GCMS).

Global Coherence Monitoring System (GCMS)

The GCMS is a worldwide network of ultra-sensitive magnetometers, designed to continuously measure magnetic signals that occur in the same range as human physiological frequencies, including our brain and heart rhythms. It is the first global network of GPS time-synchronized geomagnetic field detectors that track and measure resonances and fluctuations in the fields caused by solar storms, changes in solar wind speed, other magnetic field disruptions and, potentially, major global events that have a strong emotional component. As of this writing, there are six sensor sites located in Northern New Zealand; Boulder Creek, California; Hofuf, Saudi Arabia; Alberta, Canada; Baisogala, Lithuania; and Bonamanzi Game Park, South Africa. The GCMS will eventually expand to approximately 12 sensor sites. Each site collects continuous data that enables us to research how the fields affect human mental and emotional processes, health outcomes, and collective behaviors. GCMS technology will also enable the research teams to explore how collective human emotional states, meditations and intentions may be reflected in the earth's fields. In addition, we hope to investigate if changes in the earth's magnetic fields occur before natural catastrophes, like earthquakes and volcanic eruptions, or human events that have a strong global emotional impact, such as a social crisis or terrorist attack.

Although scientists have previously looked at some of the possible interactions between the earth's fields and human, animal and plant activity, data coming from GCI research studies and the GCMS are showing that we may be more deeply interconnected with the earth's fields than previously seen. The figure below shows an example of Earth's field line resonances, recorded at the GCMS site in Boulder Creek, California.

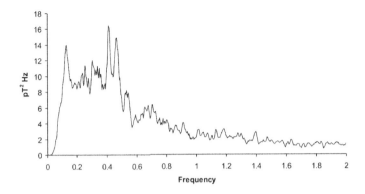

Figure 1 - The frequencies of these particular field line resonances are in the same range as many of the rhythms found
in human and animal cardiovascular and autonomic nervous-
system functions. In this Boulder Creek GCMS site graph, there
is a clear frequency at 0.1 hertz (the same frequency as the
heart rhythm in a heart coherent state). Most mathematical
models show that the resonance frequency of the human cardiovascular system is determined by feedback loops between
the heart and brain. In humans and in many animals, the resonance frequency of the system is approximately 0.1 Hz.

If the GCI hypothesis that Earth's magnetic fields are
a carrier of information that connects all living systems
proves true, it will help people understand how indi-

vidually and collectively we are affecting a global information field. That our attitudes, emotions and intentions matter and can affect all life on Earth *and that coherent, cooperative intent could impact global events and improve the quality of life on Earth.* It suggests that when large numbers of people respond to a global event with common emotional feeling, their collective response can have an effect on the quality of information distributed in the earth's field. In cases where the event evokes a negative or fearful emotional response, this can be thought of as a planetary stress wave (of information), and in cases where a positive emotional response is evoked, it could create a planetary coherence wave. One of GCI's goals is to research whether large numbers of people generating heart coherent states of love, care, appreciation and compassion can build a coherent field environment and a mutually beneficial feedback loop between people and the earth itself, creating *global coherence.*

Interconnectivity Research

One of our interconnectivity studies involved 1,600 Global Coherence Initiative members from countries around the world. The main goal of the study was to see if there were correlations that would indicate an interconnectedness study with groups of participants located near four sites around the globe where we have Global Coherence Monitoring System sensors. Six scales were used: Positive Affect/Positive Feelings, Well-Being, Anxiety, Confusion, Fatigue and Physical Symptoms. The study found that as solar wind speed and polar cap activity increased, Positive Affect/Positive Feelings and Well-Being decreased and Anxiety, Confusion and Fatigue increased.[11] Additional studies involved groups of participants wearing heart rate variability (HRV) recorders over long time periods to determine how solar and Earth magnetic fields affect autonomic nervous system functioning. One surprise was that certain solar radio changes and lower magnetic field disturbances evoked a positive nervous system response. Mental clarity increased and people felt better. An even more surprising finding from the data was an indication that human beings apparently are synchronizing at a deep level to an external signal in Earth's magnetic field environment.

The results of these studies should be published in 2016. We have recently completed the next phase of this research, which was to conduct an interconnectedness study multiple sites with groups of participants located near four locations around the globe where we have Global Coherence Monitoring System sensor sites: Saudi Arabia, Lithuania, New Zealand and California. Participants near each location were coordinated to record their HRV over the same time period. Analyzing the data will allow us to determine if the synchronization between participants and Earth is occurring both locally and globally.

The potential for creating increased coherence in *the global information field* is that it will enable us to *draw in nonlocal intuition for breakthroughs and new synergies that accelerate intuitive problem solving for addressing our social, environmental and economic challenges.*

GCI Ambassadors

Tens of thousands of people from over 150 countries have become GCI ambassadors to help co-create a better world through sending collective love and compassion into the global field environment. GCI ambassadors can join together in a Global Care Room on the GCI website (www.heartmath.org/gci) as they send heart-focused energy to the planet to help raise the vibratory rate or send care and compassion to high stress areas to help lessen the suffering of people, especially during times of crisis. Due to the increased disruptions, stress and pain that many people are experiencing throughout the world, sending compassion is one of the highest forms of love we can give to help people restore and rebalance their system.

The Global Care Room has several interesting features. When you log in to the Care Room, you see a beautiful globe of planet Earth. You see a green marker on the globe where your Internet provider is located and gold markers of all the other people around the world who are participating in the Care Room at that time. It's a refreshing experience to see gold light points representing people across the world who are coming together to connect in the heart at the same time. It is inspirational to know that a gold marker can represent a person, family or a large group of people who are doing a "Care Focus" together. Seeing this image—our Earth and people from all around the world there with you/me at the same moment—offers a powerful feeling of heart connection.

In the Global Care Room you can also leave a comment and read comments from others. Seeing someone from Malta sharing something similar to a person from Singapore or Saudi Arabia, who in turn are making inspirational comments that resonate with a person in Australia, shows that people all over the world care about creating a heart-coherent energetic field on Earth. It helps confirm the global nature of a planetary shift in action. Anyone can participate in the Global Care Room as a Guest or as a GCI Ambassador and everyone's heart energy counts.

GCI Ambassadors also commit to practicing heart coherence techniques and radiating compassion and care out to the planet. Because of increasing time pressures these days, GCI does not require specific time commitments. GCI Ambassadors determine how much time and energy and when they can contribute to a Care Focus or to radiate compassion to the planet. Using emWave or Inner Balance heart coherence feedback technology is not at all required, but is recommended for two reasons: It helps you track and increase your personal coherence baseline, which raises the community's collective coherence; and it enables you to participate in GCI research studies that require objective measures of the participants' coherence levels.

GCI's Introductory Heart Coherence Technique

Use the Heart Coherence Technique often to increase and sustain your personal coherence. Here are the six steps of this powerful tool:

✦ Breathe and calm yourself in whatever ways you choose.

✦ Choose something you appreciate—a person, pet, nature, etc., and radiate the feeling of appreciation to them for about two minutes. This helps open the heart more and increases your effectiveness when you start sending care to the planet or to a situation that needs it.

✦ Evoke a genuine feeling of compassion and care for the planet.

✦ Breathe the feelings of compassion and care going out from your heart. *(To help with focus, some imagine the compassion and care flowing out the way a river flows out to the sea. Others imagine their compassion radiating as a beam of light, or they radiate it out with the rhythm of their breath. Determine what is right for you.)*

✦ Radiate the genuine feelings of compassion and care to the planet or to a specific area of immediate need.

✦ See yourself joining with other caretakers to participate in the healing process and generating peace.

How long should you do the Heart Coherence Technique? You decide. Most people practice this technique at least five minutes a day to build personal coherence. The amount of time often increases for people when they begin to understand and experience the carryover effect and the benefits of coherence for themselves and others. Depending on your schedule, you likely will spend more time some days than others.

An Iterative Process

As we increase our personal coherence we become more sensitive to our heart's signals. When we act more often on what our heart intelligence is saying, our heart's signals get stronger and clearer. In Chapter 2 we mentioned the seminal work of John and Beatrice Lacey on heart-brain interactions. Joseph Chilton Pearce quotes the Lacey's in his book *Evolution's End*[14] (p. 103): *"Our brain sends a running report of our environmental situation to the heart, and the heart exhorts the brain to make a proper response."* GCI's theory is that increased *individual coherence* leads to increased *social coherence*, which in turn leads to increased *global coherence* in an *iterative process*.

As the iterative process spirals up, it generates a higher vibrational consciousness field that couples with the earth's information fields to accelerate individual, social and global coherence and resonance. If this theory proves true, it will support co-creative alliances and empower us as a species to serve as caretakers for our planet and generations to come. In time, global coherence will be reflected in leaders and countries adopting a more coherent global view. At this scale, and from this level of consciousness, social and economic oppression, warfare, cultural intolerance, crime and disregard for the environment can be addressed meaningfully and successfully. As the often repeated quote of Albert Einstein says, *"No problem can be solved from the same level of consciousness that created it."* Now more than ever, people are experiencing the desire to raise the vibration of their consciousness and they conveniently have all of the directions within them.

GCI Model of Change

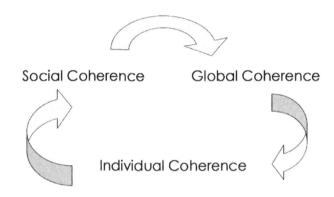

Social Coherence   Global Coherence

Individual Coherence

Heart Coherence - A Doorway to Heart-Based Living

At HeartMath we use the phrase heart-based living as a "street" term for coherent living. The term *heart-based* is randomly used by many people as a generic reference to "leading with the heart" or something similar. We didn't coin the term but we like it because it's easy to say and it casually projects its meaning. HeartMath is only one of many systems and practices that promote heart-based living. There are numerous taglines and expressions which refer to living from the heart; but regardless of what label we put on it, practicing it can make a life changing difference. Most of us sense that profound societal changes will continue to take place as our world becomes increasingly inter-connected and interdependent. Increasing our heart coherence can support a new world with more collab-oration, along with more authentic love, care and compassion.

1.	McCraty, R., Childre, D, Coherence: Bridging Personal, Social and Global Health. Alternative Therapies in Health and Medicine, 2010. 16(4): p. 10-24.

2.	Hagelin, J.S., Orme-Johnson, D. W., Rainforth, M., Cavanaugh, K., & Alexander, C. N. , Results of the National Demonstration Project to Reduce Violent Crime and Improve Governmental Effectiveness in Washington, D.C. Social Indicators Research, 1999. 47: p. 153-201.

3.	Davies, J.L., Alleviating political violence through enhancing coherence in collective consciousness: Impact assessment analysis of the Lebanon war. Dissertation Abstracts International, 1988. 49(8): p. 2381A.

4.	Orme-Johnson, D.W., et al., International Peace Project in the Middle East THE EFFECTS OF THE MAHARISHI TECHNOLOGY OF THE UNIFIED FIELD The Journal of Conflict Resolution, 1988. 32(4): p. 776-812.

5.	Hagelin, J., The Power of the Collective. Shift: At the Frontier of Consciousness, 2007. 15: p. 16-20.

6.	Bohm, D., Wholeness and the Implicate Order1980, London: Routledge and Kegan Paul.

7.	McCraty, R. and A. Deyhle, The Global Coherence Initative: Investigating the Dynamic Relationship between People and Earth's Energetic Systems in Bioe-lectromagnetic and Subtle Energy Medicine, Second Edition, P.J. Rosch, Editor 2015.

8.   Doronin, V.N., Parfentev, V.A., Tleulin, S.Zh, .Namvar, R.A., Somsikov, V.M., Drobzhev, V.I. and Chemeris, A.V., Effect of variations of the geomagnetic field and solar activity on human physiological indica-tors. Biofizika, 1998. 43(4): p. 647-653.

9.   Kay, R.W., Geomagnetic Storms: Association with Incidence of Depression as Measured by Hospital Admission. British Journal of Psychiatry, 1994. 164: p. 403-409.

10.   Mikulecký, M., Solar activity, revolutions and cultural prime in the history of mankind. Neuroendocri-nology Letters, 2007. 28(6): p. 749-756.

11.   McCraty, R., The Global Coherence Initiative: Measuring Human-Earth Energetic Interactions in 3rd Heart: King of organs conference2010: Hufuf, Saudi Arabia

12.   Ertel, S., Cosmophysical correlations of crea-tive activity in cultural history. Biophysics, 1998. 43(4): p. 696-702.

13.   McCraty, R., A. Deyhle, and D. Childre, The global coherence initiative: creating a coherent plane-

tary standing wave. Glob Adv Health Med, 2012. 1(1): p. 64-77.

14.   *Pearce, J.C., Evolution's End1992, New York: HarperCollins.*

INTRODUCTION TO

DOC CHILDRE'S CHAPTERS
By Doc Childre

The rapid global changes we are experiencing can result in beneficial outcomes for the wholeness over time, but at this point in the transition, the planet and humanity seem to be clearing old energies that prevent forward movement. Most of us are individually experiencing the intensity of these changes, consciously or unconsciously. A lot of people are feeling mood swings of hope and encouragement one day, and anxiety and resignation the next. Hopefully these next chapters will show how our heart's intuitive guidance can help us navigate these times with emotional poise, along with connecting us to our higher choices and untapped potentials. We can learn how to expand into our full capacity by practicing *heart coherence,* which is the balanced alignment between our intuitive heart, mind and emotions.

I write from the tone of my beliefs and experiences, but it's important to discern your own beliefs and what's appropriate for you. Empowerment is learning to access and follow your own heart's guidance. Much of my writing is about how living from the heart raises our vibration for increased intuitive direction in all areas of life. A few of my themes include: the heart's intelligence; increased connection with our soul, true self and source; compassion and self-compassion; transforming fear; aligning with our purpose; and how to clear old energetic habits and imprints that no longer serve us. Most of the subjects covered are summarized reflections with some practical tools that support heart-based living and self-empowerment. The content covers information that's familiar to many. Yet, a refresher on these subjects often is essential to the process of merging our higher spiritual aspects and gifts with our human nature. This enables us to become our best—our real self—with the heart power to help change the world.

CHAPTER 7

RAISING OUR VIBRATION TO ACCESS OUR
HIGHER POTENTIALS

BY DOC CHILDRE

Each day we process countless *frequencies* through our mind, brain and heart, such as thoughts, feelings and emotions. Most of us have heard someone say: "We just can't communicate; we are on totally different frequencies!", or "My brother's vibes (vibrations) seem a little down today," or "The negative vibes were so thick in that room you could trip over them." Many people assume the terms *frequency* and *vibration* (vibes) are only metaphoric expressions; yet many others intuitively realize that our thoughts, feelings, emotions and intentions *are* energetic frequencies influenced by beliefs, memories, choices, environmental stimuli, and more. In this writing I'm using terms higher and lower frequency/vibrations (vibes) to describe the up and down shifts of our moods, attitudes, behaviors, disposition, etc. Sometimes we operate in a higher vibration sometimes a lower one. It varies throughout the day, week or month, depending on how well we manage our energy in response to our interactions with life, others, or within ourselves.

When our vibrations are up, our heart energy flows through our interactions. We naturally generate uplifting feelings from a more empowered demeanor: We are kinder, more gracious and we *genuinely* connect with others. We respond to stressful situations with soundness, resilience and clearer discernment. We are less vulnerable to frustration, impatience, anger, anxiety, and we feel more self-secure and less critical of others and of ourselves. We are drawn to notice nature, flowers and trees that we usually sleep-walk past, as our preoccupations rob us of this gift of conscious connection.

When our vibrations are down, we can experience separation from others due to judgments or blame, excessive worry and low self-security, along with empty care for others because of being too preoccupied with self and our story. We are quicker to become angry, impatient, frustrated—the list.

At times radical frequency shifts in our moods and perceptions cause us to feel like we are two different people in the same body. Our behaviors and responses can become significantly different depending on the frequency of our disposition—higher, lower, or bouncing in-between. In our higher vibration we don't have to *try* to be positive because uplifting feelings and thoughts automatically flow through our system. Our heart energy is more present which increases our authentic connection with others. In a lower vibration we tend to allow negative thoughts and feelings the license to roam and feed from our life force. As we *feed them life*, they are inclined to *run our life.*

The good news is that we are not predestined victims of random frequency modulations. We can learn to consciously intervene and *reset* our vibration to a higher frequency throughout the day to engage more cost-effectively with whatever comes up. That's the long way of saying that *we have choice,* and connecting with our intuitive heart's choices is the new frontier.

How living in a lower vibration (frequency) affects our well-being

More people are finding it harder to breathe-out and relax through a day without looking over their shoulder to see if everything is okay. That was one of my main challenges. For a long time I ran constant anxiety and even when life seemed great, I couldn't be at peace or feel that everything was okay. I thought a steady current of anxiety was normal and didn't bear any consequences, until my health started telling a different story. This led to a wake-up call and the realization it was my ego vanity that was creating performance-anxiety and glitchy peace. With my heart's support, I did a *reset* and started appreciating the good in my life, rather than living in suspicion of what was not.

Continuous low grade anxiety can generate a streaming energy deficit, even if we are unconscious of it. Many of us have been trapped in this lower vibration and paid the price time and time again. Operating in a lower vibration (vibe) has a numbing effect and we fail to see the red flag drop; it becomes our *perception of reality* and we forget that we *can change* how we respond to the scenes of our life. We can't prevent all unpleasant situations that come our way, but we are responsible for how we handle them. Yet, we get so acclimatized to lower emotional habits that they feel permissible and *not accountable.* These cumulative stress deficits *are* accountable and become catalysts for accelerated aging, health issues and spiritual dismay.

External stressors, such as financial and survival pressures, health problems, work-related challenges, relationship problems—these are some of the standard triggers that lure our thoughts and feelings into a lower vibration and ramp up the stress. When our vibes are low, our feelings become lackluster as does our connection with others. There are more mistakes and do-overs; we tend to make shortsighted choices in our personal and business life, along with experiencing low to high anxiety which fuels insecurities. This can eventuate into different degrees of depression, brain fog, and fading confidence. When we don't choose to raise the vibration of our disposition, we can stay trapped for days or months in predictable stress-producing patterns that become our norm, not realizing that we are creating our own resistances. Being stuck in these patterns withers our quality of life while keeping us hamster-hiking on the same old "dread-mill"—and blaming others because it squeaks.

Our thoughts and feelings influence the chemistry that regulates much of our health—how we feel, for better or worse. We can begin to turn these energy deficits around as we realize that our thoughts, feelings, emotions and attitudes are just *frequencies* that can be changed—once we put our heart into our intention. From kids through adulthood we've been told to "put your heart into it" when pursuing matters important to us. This is because at subjective levels we instinctively know that the power of our heart's commitment can often defy odds and triumph in seemingly unachievable situations.

Heart qualities for Self-transformation

We often hear that we only use a small percent of our brain. Wait until science realizes what a small percentage of our heart's potential we utilize. One of the aims of HeartMath research is to help verify this, along with facilitating easier ways to access the endless benefits of our heart's intelligent guidance. The good news is that we don't have to wait for the blessing of science before we can draw unlimited benefits from our intuitive heart's guidance.

Old, unwanted habit patterns change more gracefully as our heart and mind partner in supporting our commitments. For most of us, deeper emotional imprints from the past are harder to change. Sometimes it's helpful to address them a little at a time, in segments. Stuck emotional patterns can be similar to rusted bolts that require being soaked in solvent to dissolve the resistance. Accepting our difficulties gracefully is a powerful solvent which frees up our heart's intuitive insight for helping us handle more effectively whatever challenges life brings.

Making peace with our resistances gets easier as we learn that much of our lack of peace comes from the unmanaged significance we assign to issues. For example: It's increased significance that turns a simple concern into obsessive worry, or turns a little anxiety into pressing fear. Unbridled significance over-swells the size of our challenges, especially emotional challenges. Excessive significance and drama create doubt in our capacity to cope, which sparks low grade or high intensity anxiety. We can learn to consciously reduce the significance we feed lower thought frequencies and stop this piracy of our personal vitality and peace. Practicing self-compassion (not self-pity) creates a soaking effect that reduces the emotional significance that blocks clear assessment for better options. As we reduce significance, we are quickly rewarded because it doesn't take long to see the payoff.

We often make high-spirited commitments for behavior changes and then get stuck from not having the patience, self-acceptance and self-compassion to support our process of change. We forget to use these transformational heart qualities right at the time they would benefit us the most. Don't feel awkward about giving yourself care and compassion; there's enough to go around—you can have your cake and eat it too in this situation. At the core level we are caring beings, regardless of the veneer and cloaking behaviors we've picked up along the way. The collective heart awakening on the planet is nudging us to remove our mask and start showing up more as who we are.

Rushed energy

Rushed, impatient energy diffuses our capacity for favorable outcomes when we're involved in sensitive discernments regarding choices. When we push energy, this cancels the experience of flow and creates hiccups in our intentions. Patience and ease actually create the energetic environment for flow to take place in our communications, choice selections and actions. It's our mind that tends to rush energy; our heart chooses balance, rhythm and flow. When cooperating together they increase outcomes that fit the need of the situation.

The partnership between our mind and heart expands our capacity to experience life's interactions with more rhythm and flow. Rhythm has to do with the timing and sensitivity in our engagements. (It's similar to the way physical rhythm helps minimize the clunks in our dance steps.) In high school I remember pushing energy trying to learn complex dance steps in the Irish Jig, and the more I pushed the more I was fussed at by my teacher. The more I was fussed at, the harder I pushed, and the more I clunked until I was put on the second-string dance team. The teacher explained that I was pushing so hard from the mind to learn the steps that it blocked me from learning a most important part–the rhythm.

As I grew up, I saw this play out in many life situations where people trip over themselves from pushing energy against flow (like swimming upstream). The magic from applying balance, rhythm and flow is that it prevents and dissolves stress and resistances while on the move. This becomes *an advantage leap* once we understand the importance of internal energy economy.

Shifting lower attitude frequencies

We're all aware that certain attitudes or tendencies can be tougher to shift. But the process becomes easier once our mind agrees to cooperate more harmoniously with our heart's intuitive feelings. More people are intuitively sensing that they have the capacity to re-write depleting emotional behavior patterns. When our mind's perception aligns with our heart's intuitive assessment, then a bigger picture is seen and new possibilities emerge.

Attitudes and perceptions are like pre-set frequencies that we store and activate at times, depending on how we feel or if we are in a higher or lower vibration. Most all of us have practiced maintaining an uplifting attitude as this allows more access to the "flow" in our interactions. Often, when we are challenged by a decision, someone tells us, "Relax, you have choices." However, when we are operating in our lower frequency attitude, we filter out our most *effective choices* and perceptions. We tend to only see *inferior choices* and we go with them, time and time again repeating the same lessons unlearned. We often have to repeat our lessons before we attain the take-home value. When tired of learning the same lessons, we can connect with our heart and take responsibility, bypass the drama and blame, and move forward with what we've learned. Sometimes this flows smoothly, and sometimes the moving parts grind a little through the transition.

Negative thoughts and feelings

At times random negative thoughts stream through us all. Many of these thoughts and feelings can pass quickly if we reduce the drama and significance we assign to them. We are not bad for having negative thoughts, but we can refuse to become a yoyo-bot of their stressful creations. There are many energy leaks that lower our vibration and performance, such as irritation, impatience, frustration, etc. These *assumed* small energy leaks, such as impatience for example, often turn into blockbuster energy deficits over time if we don't reset and transform them into a higher vibration—like patience, resilience and flow. These addictive low vibrational habits restrict our flow of spirit, which eventually creates glitches in our major operating systems—mental, emotional, physical (nervous system and more). This increases our vulnerability to the standard health problems experienced from constant overload in our emotional system.

As we genuinely desire it, our *heart's intuitive prompter* will begin to signal us when our vibration is low and we are spiraling into a stress deficit from energy drain. The signal from our heart's intuitive prompter becomes clearer as we use it. It alerts us when we are seduced back into old patterns that are not who we choose to be, and supports us in re-firing our healthy commitments and attitudes. Most of us are connected with our heart's prompter to some degree. This connection progressively opens the door for receiving our inner guidance. Some of us know from experience that intuition is more likely to jam up when approached from a desperate mind, but is more accessible in the stillness of a calm and open heart.

Quick exercise for replacing lower frequency feelings

The following short and simple exercise can be helpful in replacing lower frequency feelings. (It's similar to the "Overcare Exercise" provided in a later chapter.)

1. Pick a time when you feel sad or insecure, disconnected from others, or any lower vibrational feelings you would want to replace and feel better.

2. Find a place to breathe quietly for a few minutes and with each breath imagine your mind, emotions and body getting still inside.

3. From that place of stillness, imagine the kind of feeling you would like to have, or have felt before when you were more self-secure. As you breathe, imagine that you are breathing this new feeling into your being.

4. The last step is to breathe this feeling a few minutes to anchor it. Try it again later if it doesn't work. Sometimes we give up too quickly on the things that would benefit us the most.

It's helpful to remember that small children often use their imagination to *quickly* transform their feelings from anger and frustration into elation and happiness. We have this capacity as adults too, but we accumulate so many handed down mind-driven programs, that it creates a decline in the direct heart connection and emotional resilience we had as kids. As adults we usually have to practice with commitment to reawaken this direct connection to our heart's intelligence, and then integrate it into our interactions. This creates more balanced decisions and a straighter path to our best outcomes.

Practice shifting small unwanted feelings and eventually you'll find yourself replacing stronger feelings, habits and mindsets. The door to the hidden power of our heart can be opened, but sometimes we have to jiggle the handle a few times to loosen up the old habit of resistance.

More tips to raise your frequency pitch

Re-connecting with heart feelings throughout the day, such as gratitude, kindness, compassion, patience and flow, keeps our vibration up while preventing and eliminating many merry-go-round energy deficits. These heart qualities serve to facilitate our overall health and wellbeing.

Another effective way to raise our frequency pitch/vibration is to take a few days and appreciate connections and friendships that we have adapted to or unintentionally taken for granted. *Adapting* creeps into our relationships in a stealthy, hard-to-recognize, fashion. Then it quietly reduces the warmth and the "zing" in our connections. Take a heart stand not to let caring relationships wilt from adapting! As we make appreciation and gratitude *a way of life*, this offsets adapting and keeps the spirit within our connections alive and self-replenishing. Gratitude and kindness are two of *love's* most magnetic expressions which draw to us the highest best that life has to offer.

The higher vibration of our true self naturally generates the textures of kindness and respect and other qualities which are core heart frequencies that harmonize our life's exchanges. Heart textures such as gratitude and compassion naturally radiate from us when our heart is engaged in our connections and communication. Humanity is evolving past *pilot-light care* (low heart warmth*)*, which only produces surface level interactions that are missing the regenerative benefits of authentic connection.

In general, our hearts are warmer to our family, pets and our circle of friends. As we spiritually mature, our heart warmth expands to include more people in its care; our respect for nature increases. We begin to desire being part of something that makes a difference—something that serves the greater whole of humanity. From there our love matures into unconditional love, without borders. In this vibration we are more directly connected with our heart's intuitive guidance for creating joy and fulfillment while supporting others to do the same. We can shorten the time this takes by learning to connect with our heart's intelligent guidance.

Many books and articles have been written on the efficacy of practicing the core qualities of the heart. These primary attributes not only raise our personal vibration, they help to lift the environmental vibration as well. We spiritually prosper each time we refresh these natural transforming heart qualities. Don't think of your practice as a discipline; see it as a free pass to your own high-end health spa with guaranteed beneficial results.

The active ingredients in prayer and meditation

One of the major subjective values of *heart-connected* prayers or meditations is that they often leave us with a feeling of warmth and confirmation. Even if we don't get a direct linear answer, we don't judge our soul or source as much for being too busy with others to answer our calls (like I used to do as a teenager). More and more people are exploring a deeper connection with their heart because it doesn't take away or compete with their religion, spiritual path, or basic belief system. It strengthens it. Most of us can agree that whatever spiritual practice we choose, it's important to add the qualities of our own heart's guidance to the mix.

Being genuine and heart-connected with your feelings provides the activating ingredients in prayer, meditation, etc. We all have felt the obvious difference between genuine appreciation and counterfeit appreciation. When appreciation is not genuine, it's not real – it's no more effective than a "store mannequin" trying to appreciate window shoppers. For instance, when blessing our food, we know the difference when we are heart-connected or when we are mechanically repeating a memorized prayer (while worrying if we are going to get a homemade biscuit because half of the soccer team suddenly showed up hungry, unannounced). When prayers and meditations run split screens with other preoccupations, this won't raise our vibration and we usually end up with wasted time filled with unfocused mind traffic.

Stillness

Many spiritual cultures agree that *inner stillness* creates an energetic environment for supporting our advancing consciousness which can unleash the transformational power of our love. That's why from the beginning of HeartMath, many of the tools and especially the technology have been designed to monitor and facilitate easier access to stillness and its connection to our natural inner wisdom and guidance. Forget the mystical and think of inner stillness as something practical and street worthy. How many times have we told friends or children to *get still inside* and listen up because we have something important to tell them? This reveals our innate respect for the value of stillness, so why not use it the way it can count the most—to quiet our mental and emotional static so that we can hear the council from our larger self.

When our mind finally lets go, inner stillness is where we land. From there we can reset and upgrade the experience of our life. The earlier we learn the value of inner stillness, the less we need to experience the firmer ways life nudges us into considering higher choices for personal peace and happiness. We often hear ourselves and others say, "If I had more *foresight*, I would have handled that situation differently." Stillness is a primary source for increasing our foresight and discernment. Inner stillness is a place that our heart can speak without the mind running it off the road. In order to "be still, and know" we first have to be still enough to listen.

It's a forward moving choice to schedule times for inner stillness and allow our heart, mind and emotions to experience a *time-out* from competing with each other and enjoy some casual peace together. Stillness requires a little practice because our mind will try to occupy that space (or any space if the door is left cracked).

If inner stillness didn't produce high-value results, think of all the centuries of *time* that meditators and spiritually conscious people would have wasted throughout history. With refinement, inner stillness becomes like a personal elevator to our highest view and eliminates the weariness from climbing endless stairs. I feel that practicing inner stillness to connect with our heart's intelligent guidance will become a most positive corner-turning step forward for humanity, not as a trend or religious motivation but as a street sense, heart-based way of life.

How do we take the benefits from our inner stillness meditations and prayers into our day to day activities? Operating from a *state of ease* is a natural practice for bringing the essence of stillness into our daily interactive mode. (*Practicing the state of ease and its benefits in these times is discussed thoroughly in the next chapter.*) We can learn to do this by breathing the attitude of *ease* at times throughout the day. Breathing the attitude of ease helps us to step down the carry-over effects of our inner stillness meditations into our normal interactions and activities. When we discern our direction from a place of inner ease, this helps to prevent the impatience of our mind from overriding the intuitive whispers of our higher choices. Acting from a place of inner ease is a heart intelligent skill in the economy of personal energy management and distribution. This practice reduces many decision-making regrets and also helps to access the magic of flow in our processes. Flow provides the straightest line to manifesting our intentions.

Heart Intuition

Connecting with our heart's intuition (inner guid-ance) from a place of stillness can advance our capacity to take charge of our life's decisions and direction. Our spiritual heart is a most beneficial, yet under-used as-pect of our true nature and potentials. When our mind is not partnering with our heart, it often favors our ego's choices in decisions, more than supporting the highest outcome for all concerned. This pattern accu-mulates an energy deficit that feeds back in our physi-cal and emotional system. Then our vibration drops and we target something to blame other than us.

A helpful way to encourage intuitive connection is to soften our posture on *knowing what we know* too quickly about everything. As my self-awareness in-creased, I realized that I was crafty at blocking my intu-ition so it wouldn't compete with my "made up mind" about what I wanted. Then I realized most of humanity is also good at that, which is one of the biggest reasons intuition hasn't made its way into the mainstream as a most intelligent, personal guidance system. It's hu-morous how often *we reject our heart's intuitive feel-*

ings and go with our ego choices, and then we take meditation classes—*hoping to develop intuitive guidance.*

Our intuitive heart can foresee our higher outcome options and offer our mind and emotions better choices for navigating life's situations. Deep heart listening in stillness can create the energetic link to the wisdom and directions from our true self, soul, or our connection with source. *(Insert your own preferred names for these higher vibrational states, such as soul, true self, source, etc., based on your cultural beliefs, studies or experiences.)* Getting these names right to suit ourselves or others is not as important in the process of moving forward spiritually as one might think. For convenience, I often bundle them all together and refer to them as *"my large."* For example, if a resistance comes up in my life, I simply get still in my heart and connect with *my large* for effective suggestions.

In times past, I searched unceasingly for the magic of intuitive access, the glamorous aspects—psychic abilities, seeing the future, lottery numbers, etc., rather than looking for inner guidance, deeper discernment and grounded choices. It's normal to desire that which coddles the ego when we first get enamored with intuition and its possibilities. Later, stress from health problems influenced me to explore intuition more for insights regarding my day-to-day choices and ways to serve humanity. As we put first things first, then the extras can naturally unfold as add-ons to our fulfillment, but not a driving force that decides our fulfillment.

With that said, I still could enjoy winning a mega-million dollar lottery and heading straight to the local "Dollar Store" to do some serious binge shopping ...without having to glance at the price tags! Afterwards I would stop by the local Bentley/Rolls Royce dealership and order a humble, run-about model. *(This is meant as twisty humor regarding the vanities of apologetic abundance.)* We don't have to feel apologetic if our personal abundance includes fine things. Many people know this at the conceptual level, but for some, their emotions are still trapped in shades of guilt—causing them to experience abundance through a restricted state of enjoyment. If you are experiencing this, it's time to lose those restrictions and quit punishing your joy.

Our Inner Dignity

True dignity, not pretended, is a powerful heart frequency that supports the maintenance of inner-composure, especially when the tone of our interactions starts to compromise our integrity. At times we can feel exhausted and insecure from the weight of change, and that's understandable. This is a perfect opportunity to renew our dignity and practice self-compassion to replenish our resilience—especially when life presses us with choices faster than our capacity to sort out our moves. When holding the vibration of dignity and poise, we are more effective at preventing and reducing incessant worry (hurried aging). Our minds have tried endlessly to legalize worry, yet the intelligence within our core heart occasionally informs us that worry is a stress accelerator which feeds on our wholeness health. Worry is discussed more in the "Care and Overcare" chapter.

True Self

Our true self represents an achievable vibration within us that contains the wisdom and intelligence of our heart. In this higher vibration, we are harmoniously connected with the hearts of others and all life. We naturally exude unconditional love and compassion that's not diluted from over-attachment to others, issues or outcomes. Our spiritual advancement is not dignified by trying to be perfect or being exempt from learning and growing. Accepting our fallibility is a leap towards becoming authentic. Increased authenticity unfolds as we raise the vibration of our life with heart-felt connections, non-judgment and acceptance, while including ourselves in our love.

Operating continuously in the higher vibration of our true self is not expected of us overnight. It's a process that unfolds at the rate-of-genuine commitment—if we don't waste our spunk peeping over our shoulder to gloat at our progress. When we over-analyze progress we risk stopping it in its tracks, especially if it's used just for ego inflation. Increasingly, more of us now desire to reset our life with a fresh start by leading with the heart and proceeding with love in areas that we normally keep roped off. We have our reasons for keeping our heart at arm's length from others, but maybe it's time to challenge these reasons to see if they are handed down behaviors that don't represent who we really are.

Humanity is transitioning into a state of consciousness that will unleash the creative power of togetherness, and the understanding that it's our heart vibration that qualifies the difference between separation and feeling connected. Increased heart-connected interactions will progressively raise the vibration of collective consciousness. This will set the stage for realizing that inclusive, unconditional love and compassion is the next advanced mode of intelligent living. Millions of people, and consistently more, will be benefiting from this new awareness long before the whole of humanity chooses it. Individual choices and timing have to be allowed without judgment and condescension. As more of us practice operating from our true self, the restorative power of our collective compassion naturally increases. This will make it easier for others to free themselves from limited beliefs that repress the human potentials which reside in the hidden power of the heart. The door to the global heart is opening and I suggest that love will increasingly pour its way through the streets.

CHAPTER 8

MOVING IN A STATE OF EASE
By Doc Childre

"Ease" is an inner state that helps us transit more smoothly through the energies and rhythms of our life's experiences. Operating in the state of inner ease allows us easier connection with our heart's intuitive guidance to provide creative ideas, practical solutions or effective options for responding to most situations.

Many people conceptually understand the value of ease, but our pressing minds and emotions tend to override the wisdom to actually practice it, especially when deeper discernment and wiser choices are needed. As the speed of life keeps accelerating, the mind and emotions can become overstretched from having to make decisions and choices too quickly due to the pressures of responsibilities and commitments. Even the "Now" seems to have sped up—it used to last a full moment but I think that extra time is shrinking.

The practice of "breathing ease" helps to slow down the vibratory rate of the mind and emotions so our heart's intuitive input can weigh in on choices and actions. In most cases, the speed and aggression of the mind and emotions drown out our heart's feelings and intuitive guidance. Inner ease creates a receptive space for intuitive suggestions and feelings that are broadcast from our heart's intelligence. Ease doesn't drag our thinking down; it clears it up.

Several HeartMath research studies have confirmed the benefits of practicing ease. In these studies, breathing ease played a pivotal role in helping participants slow the vibrations of the mind and emotions so that the heart's intuitive feelings could be translated into higher reasoning and choices.

Let's take a deeper look at a few of the ways that people already naturally use ease in daily life, along with some advanced ways to use it for achieving desired outcomes. This will help to broaden our understanding and respect for the benefits and advantages of this common sense practice.

At times we tell children and friends to ease up and pay close attention. This is because deep inside we intuitively know that when people ease the vibration of their mind and emotions, they listen smarter, they hear deeper, they comprehend what they hear, they leave you feeling heard—which is a rare treat nowadays. (The humor is that we can feel the benefits and intelligence of ease when others are listening from that place, yet we can go a year and not think about "easing up" on ourselves in our interactions.)

It's important to note that ease is not a floaty-blissy or sleepy-headed state. I know the term "ease" sounds soft, like a butterfly practicing ballet or such, but don't underestimate its power of effectiveness.

Highly trained athletes can run races while maintaining a state of ease in their mind and emotions. Olympic athletes especially know that when their mind and emotions are at ease and in check, it enables a resonant alignment between heart, mind and emotions which bolsters their power to achieve their aim. This results in higher scores and outcomes. Also, when we are in the state of ease our emotions rebound quicker if disappointments or setbacks occur, which is important.

Navy Seals and other Special Forces units utilize HeartMath's emWave coherence technology for increasing personal coherence which helps sustain a state of inner ease. This practice increases alertness and receptivity to intuitive input when discerning critical situations and choices.

People tell each other at times to "ease up and find the flow." An advanced practice for finding the flow is learning to create the flow, especially in non-flowing situations. We have the power in our hearts to do this. When a seasoned surfer experiences the flow, it's not dependent on having perfect waves—flow is especially about how gracefully she adjusts to daunting waves or turbulent weather. She is poised in inner balance and creates her own flow to suit each environmental circumstance.

We all are constantly surfing through life's potentials along with its challenges and inconsistencies. How we greet them decides our ratio of flow or how much stress we accumulate from situational resistances. Practicing ease creates flow by helping to regulate the balance and cooperation between our heart, mind and emotions (coherence).

Each day people are telling each other to "just breathe". What we're saying is yes, breathe, but add the attitude of calm and ease as you breathe, which can help quieten the mind and emotions—so that intuitive guidance can be accessed. It's important to learn to feel when you really are in ease instead of assuming it. Breathing inner ease throughout the day will help anchor the pattern into your cellular memory. With practice, you will find this increasingly helpful for stabilizing your emotions and maintaining your balance.

Again all I mean by breathing ease is: As you casually breathe, imagine breathing in the attitude of calm and ease—the same way we tell kids to do.

Some examples of times to breathe ease for a while:

When you want to prevent or reduce anxiety.

When you get caught in a drama-fest type of situation. (Breathing ease helps you remember that if you can't leave the situation, you can practice being "in" it, but not "of" it.)

To prevent or restore energetic composure from overwhelm.

Before and during meetings. (Breathing the attitude of ease sets an internal environment for deeper listening, better comprehension and staying emotionally poised. However, if your composure crashes, ease helps you re-center quicker, especially if you are caught in a heated dispute.)

Before you respond to a vexing e-mail, breathe ease and settle the mind and emotions. (You can often prevent an emotional mess and the downtime it takes for damage control.)

To access or restore patience and resilience whenever needed. (Ease is usually the missing ingredient when we are impatient. Breathing ease creates the tolerance that disarms impatience.)

While discerning important issues or choices. To slow down your mental and emotional traffic so that intuitive insight can be perceived.

When you want to be creative, as ease draws (or unleashes) intuitive direction.

Before sleep if you have sleep problems.

When life's challenges are coming in faster than solutions.

During times of global uncertainty, rapid planetary changes and increased electromagnetic or solar activity, practicing inner ease will save a lot of energy, angst and downtime. These environmental influences can trigger increased excitability, which may affect our mental/emotional behavior patterns in unexpected ways (memory lapses, brain fog, anxiety, explosive emotions, edginess, aches in odd places, sleeplessness, elation, depression and more). When you experience these symptoms, it's helpful to breathe ease and take deeper pause for discerning and double-checking communications and decisions. Take life a segment at a time and practice discerning your steps from the place of inner ease which translates into more reliable choices and better health from the stress you avoid.

For many of us, knowing how to access inner ease is not the problem—it's remembering to do it, especially when it counts the most. This gives us a chance to act and respond from our real self rather than from our mechanical, "predictable other." Ease is a higher vibrational gift from the intelligence of our heart.

CHAPTER 9

OUR SOUL CONNECTION
AND FINDING OUR PURPOSE
By Doc Childre

There are countless beliefs and theories regarding the soul, source, higher self, etc. None of these have been scientifically proven. If such terms don't resonate with your perceptions and beliefs, you can disregard them because this won't hinder your progress along the path to becoming who you truly are. Know that you don't have to totally understand the soul or believe it exists to receive its benefits. Your own spirit will bring you the understanding of your soul and true self and their higher potentials in perfect timing.

Many people practice care, compassion, kindness and other expressions of love, though they don't believe in or choose to be involved in teachings concerning the soul or the *source* of existence. Becoming self-responsible and serving the greater whole through love can expand our peace and happiness, even if we don't choose to put name-tags on where this energy came from.

The next paragraphs regarding the soul are my personal beliefs and perceptions from my experiences and studies. These work for me now but I've learned many times over not to seal the door to expanding or modifying my beliefs. Allow your own inner guidance to discern your personal perceptions and feelings concerning the soul and true self. It's prudent not to agree with my perceptions (or anyone's) regarding soul, source, true self, or anything else I've written about without assessing it through your own deep heart feelings and discernment. Nowadays it's important for individuals to increasingly rely on their own evaluation, especially with the flood of new information emerging which explores spirituality, consciousness, inner and outer space, and such. We can all expect that our perceptions and formulations will change a few times along the way as our awareness expands.

Living from our heart develops resonance and cooperation between our heart, mind, brain and emotions. When these powerful energies are not resonating as a team, and have opposing desires and agendas, this generates much (or most) of our stress accumulation. These divisions in our operating system create incoherence which represses the spirit and heart energy that supply our joy and sense of wellbeing. When our heart energy is low, we feel less care, kindness and connection with others and scattered within ourselves. Our attempts at happiness are often half-baked with little feeling and are vulnerable to constant disruption. We can change this pattern as we understand the value of coherence and use it to realign our mind and emotions with our heart a few times throughout the day. Practicing heart coherence is important at any time for boosting intuitive connection, resilience and emotional balance, especially during times of personal or global stress. Our soul nudges and supports us in becoming more coherent as this is the optimum frequency and vibration for creating harmony, better choices and fulfillment. Coherence is also the baseline for wholeness healing practices.

I perceive that the soul and true self are aspects of our being that vibrate at a higher frequency of consciousness than our standard human awareness—until our awareness merges with that higher vibration over time. My perception is that humanity's collective purpose is to raise the vibration of consciousness. This creates an energy field that supports a coherent, harmonious foundation for creating peace and a world that thrives, not just survives. I believe that our soul's wisdom gathered from many experiences is there to facilitate us with unconditional love, healing, and intelligent direction. Also that our higher mind and heart are primary receiving stations for the wisdom and guidance from our soul, although our soul energy permeates our whole being.

For ages it's been said that within our heart our questions can be answered, along with guidance and directions for fulfillment. I suggest that this will become more accepted and increasingly validated by many individuals in the foreseeable future. Many people are already experiencing a deeper connection with their inner guidance. More are feeling increased curiosity regarding the soul, along with the nudge to connect with their heart's intelligent insights. When exploring our spiritual heart's potentials in prayer or meditation, we progressively learn to distinguish the difference between our heart's guidance and our mind's foolery. Most of us have felt the swinging-door of unsureness when discerning our inner voice; we may occasionally even wonder if our prayers and meditations ever land on anyone's desk that matters.

Discerning our heart and soul's directions and choices will refine as the sensitivity to our higher vibration increases, which it will with genuine commitment. Having a sincere heart's desire to connect with our soul vibration will help to draw its facilitation into our mental, emotional and biological systems in a more focused way. Don't expect your soul to jump out and hand you an identification card with its picture on it and ask, "How can I help you today?" Simply approach your soul connection from the heart with ease and without "Pollyanna" expectancies; this creates a resonant environment for increasing sensitivity to your soul's essence.

Our relationship to our soul becomes more effective by editing out the mystery and complexity around it. To lighten the subject: Casually imagine the soul as an integral part of our self, like a buddy that offers a handy, helicopter-view of less cluttered pathways and directions through life's opportunities or challenges. We still have to make choices, yet our higher choices become more obvious as we increase our capacity to listen in stillness to our heart's intelligent guidance.

Our heart steps down higher vibrational choices from our soul and larger self, which upgrades our awareness to move in the direction of our highest purpose. We are not chased down by our soul and wrestled into becoming little "automated do-gooders," nor does our soul police our choices and directions; its love is unconditional—it allows. The humor is that we would probably have an easier ride if our soul and true self did impose their view of higher choices.

Consciously integrating the wisdom and support from our soul into our life's interactions releases the unconditional love, compassion and heart intelligence that we already own. This practice raises our awareness to become more inclusive of the *whole of humanity,* with whom we are all energetically connected. Our soul and true self work in concert and are energetically connected with other souls. Increasing our love for each other creates easier access to our soul and our true self's assistance. I feel that *love* is the action word for achieving the next level of consciousness, and the quickest way to ascend the spiraling staircase we refer to as the path. Our soul is on stand-by to help coach this process.

Don't feel that you are unworthy of your soul's facilitation. If you are reading about or pondering the connection with your soul's guidance, you are especially ready for its extra facilitation in becoming your true self. Becoming your best involves merging with this higher vibrational aspect of yourself, which is also humanity's grand next step in consciousness expansion.

Our soul is not perched in a castle at the top of countless flights of stairs. Many of us have already climbed those stairs, and now it's time to cease the heavy lifting and find a straighter line to our soul and higher potentials. We can learn to quietly breathe our way into the *stillness* of our heart space which supports increased connection with the virtues of our soul vibration.

Here's what works for me. To ease myself into stillness, I sit for a few minutes and breathe consciously. On the in-breath, I imagine breathing in divine love throughout my being. On the out-breath, I radiate the *feeling* of gratitude. Doing this raises my vibration and helps to bring heart, mind, emotions and body into *coherent alignment* and *stillness*. This resonance creates an energetic conduit for the love and guidance from the soul and true self to integrate more easily with my normal human vibration. If you decide to try this, be patient while getting the feel of the process. Without patience, your mind will tend to expect too much too quickly and you will likely give up, disappointed.

Our soul decides the best way to facilitate us based on our highest needs, which is not always what our personality requests (though sometimes it is). We quickly figure out that our soul is not a "convenient-mart" for ego supplements; instead it helps to transform our ego-generated residues from the past. In the now, we are creating the blueprint for our future. As we progressively merge with our soul and true self, this steps up our vibration to magnetize higher outcomes and increased peace. As our soul energy becomes more present, we become more capable of manifesting our full potential. We serve others and expand our love past our small circle to include the greater collective. People are already experiencing this, especially many in the younger generation. They have their share of challenges, but seem more connected with their natural abilities, talents and gifts from their higher potentials. Soon we will need a bigger word than *talent* to define their multifaceted capacities. Actually this is already the case. We all have a special vibration that contributes to the whole when we operate from our heart space.

I feel that much of humanity will find a deeper reassuring connection with their heart's guidance, regardless of the challenges from unexpected global changes. In my life's review, it was the pressing challenges that first scooted me into my *deeper heart* connection for solutions and guidance. Like many others, I had the standard tendency to repress my heart's intuitive directions so they wouldn't supervise or hinder my mind-driven ambitions or my off-road choices. After enough emotional pain and setbacks, I finally realized that I could establish a bonded connection with my deeper heart's guidance without pain and regret often being my source of inspiration. Pain was not my preferred door to the heart, but I appreciate that it served as a door until I learned that love and kindness created a much easier entry. With meaningful intention we can all create this life changing intuitive heart connection. Expanding our love, care and kindness for others helps activate and anchor our heart's intuitive connection as a street-wise way of life, not just as a passing trend. We have a limitless supply of love within our heart and soul waiting to hit the street running.

Our soul's wisdom is similar to an *app* that's activated as we get still and log into our heart. As our heart energy becomes more present, the clarity of our intuitive messaging increases. Practicing in the vibration of love and stillness helps to tune out the *fuzzy* in our intuitive reception and comprehension.

We don't have to be book smart, tech smart or keep up with all the new spiritual trends and jargon to connect with our heart's guidance and manifest our unrealized gifts and potentials. Many systems now are pointing people to explore the natural guidance system within themselves for directions. This will continue to move into mainstream acceptance as more people spiritually mature and desire a deeper connection with their true self through their own inner resources.

HeartMath and many other systems can inspire, but you don't have to depend on them because you have the guidance within your own heart and soul connection. That's one of the most important message-themes in my writings; the rest is just "filler" information that hopefully will inspire people to explore and access the transformational assistance of their heart's intelligence.

You can use HeartMath and other helpful systems in the same way that many of us used training wheels on our bikes as kids. The training wheels helped us to connect with our sense of balance and self-possibilities but soon *we were riding on our own without the props.* Aim to unfold your own empowerment and the confidence that goes with it, and know that your contribution of love and care to the planet and all life is just as important as any other's. If you feel less than that, know that you can re-write the beliefs and mindsets that keep you in this lower vibration of self-limitation.

We are not more important than each other. Awareness varies between people because individuals have different timings for personal awareness shifts. This is based on certain life lessons to be experienced so as to free up more of the power of our love. Comparing our awareness can seduce us into feeling less or more important than others through certain stages of our unfoldment. This is a normal aspect of our ego— the vanity of being special (or not special). Our ego quietly becomes less of an issue as we become more mindful and commit to the ways of love, kindness and compassion. As we practice putting conscious care into our interactions and keep our humility refreshed, then our forward movement quickens with more flow and less resistance.

Purpose

People awakening on the path will eventually get curious about their *purpose*, as many now are experiencing. Some people grow up connected with their sense of purpose. Others have searched far and wide for teachers or signs to point them toward their purpose, while many others are not presently concerned with purpose. Early on the path our sense of purpose can bounce around and shape-shift at times. This is because, as our heart's intuition starts to increase, this raises our vibration and awareness which often changes the course of our desires and directions.

The practice of connecting with our heart's intuitive guidance is a good jump-start for unveiling purpose in perfectly timed stages of our unfoldment. After our mind surrenders the urgency to unveil our purpose, this increases the fun synchronicities that light the way. Our purpose quest becomes more adventuresome when the puzzle pieces show up through unexpected side doors.

If you are someone who follows your passions to discover purpose, it's helpful to understand that passion energy serves the highest bidder—this could be our intuitive heart's desire at times or mostly our ego-driven ambition at other times. Occasionally what we identify as our passion drive can turn out to be ego-fed energy powered by the mind without the heart's discernment. This is not always the case, but check periodically to see if that particular door is ajar. In other cases our sense of purpose is aligned with our heart's direction, but the passion seems to be missing—then the passion unfolds later after we spiritually mature a little more in certain areas of our growth.

After it dawned on me that I had been chasing my heart's purpose mostly with my mind, I finally released the glamor of being too caught up in purpose-browsing and learned to trust in my heart's guidance to help connect the dots. My heart revealed this to me: Learning to listen to my heart's guidance was *the most important step* in manifesting my purpose, regardless of how my vocational choices and life played out.

Establishing more trust in my heart's wisdom created a baseline which made it easier for my internal and external purpose to naturally align with each other through time. My passion and sense of mission increased as I matured in the way I responded to life's lessons. I was shown that another key aspect of my purpose was learning to use my heart's intelligence to help navigate the transition between self-centeredness and an expanded love for the whole. I began the process of sorting out who I am from who I thought I was. I saw that to become my true self would involve learning to free the dynamic love that I felt inside, but couldn't fully express because of my resistance to loving myself.

Years ago, the term self-love put me off, as it sounded too self-centered. My perception changed as I realized that loving myself was simply practicing natural heart qualities such as: gratitude, patience, being kinder and more compassionate with myself, including my heart more in decisions and choices, being mindful and non-judgmental of my inner and external environment, releasing the vanity around failing to get everything perfect, etc. These practices bring forth the essence of our true self. Our true self *is already perfect*; it doesn't require fixing—it's like a perfect orange that's full of sunshine but we have to take the peeling off to free up the juice. We advance as we peel off the old perceptions and behaviors that no longer benefit us and that keep people from getting along. Doing this reveals the light and gifts from our true being.

For many years now, the external manifestation of my purpose has been to make available anything I've learned that might facilitate others who choose to connect with their heart's intelligent guidance. Living from our heart connects the puzzle pieces of our purpose and aligns us with our personal empowerment and fulfillment.

Conscience

Most of us have heard this statement repeated throughout life: "Let your conscience be your guide." Our conscience signals us at times, like a text message, offering an opportunity to course-correct our attitudes or actions. Usually when someone says, "My conscience is bothering me," it's when their thoughts, feelings or actions are out of sync with the integrity of their true nature—their heart of hearts. Though our conscience doesn't force us to comply with its suggestions, it affords us a chance to think twice, and then twice again, before engaging in or continuing certain ego-driven notions that don't include our heart's assessment of the circumstances. Conscience is an intuitive vibration that serves as a reminder of our integrity, dignity and care. It's a reference of intuitive assessment, prompting us to be more conscious in discerning our choices and actions. Our conscience is a friendly, yet occasionally firm reminder of who we really are when we are dipping too low into "who we are not."

I wish the designer would have given conscience a louder voice because some of the choices I made in my twenties were proof that I could hardly hear it at all. Many people are commenting to us that their conscience is getting louder and clearer. This will increase and become more obvious as these changing times continue, and as we connect more with our heart and the care that we are about.

Balancing Masculine and Feminine Energy Within

It's often a mystery why many of our practices and intentions for self-transformation tend to fizzle. Part of the reason is because of the lack of balance and partnership between the masculine and feminine energy within each of us. Each person is a combination of masculine and feminine frequencies, regardless of their gender. For example, our *feminine* side is more sensitive to our intuitive guidance and our *masculine* energy is important for helping to step down and anchor this guidance into day-to-day behavior. This is only one example of balanced partnering between our masculine and feminine qualities.

Transformational benefits of balancing our masculine and feminine energy include a clearer connection with our heart's intelligent communication, an increased capacity to heal and maintain our system, and more. Our masculine and feminine energies (frequencies) shape our lives. Our heart's intelligence can help to unfold the balance and cooperation between these two energies that constantly fashion our outcomes and decide our peace.

The imbalance of our masculine and feminine energy results in many of the mental and emotional limitations that hinder our potential for being the best that we can be. Usually we are top-heavy on one side or the other. This imbalance weakens our self-assessment capacity, causing us to over-play our strengths so as to hide our weaknesses from others and ourselves. This is only one of many different play-outs that spin from masculine and feminine energetic imbalance. More people are feeling a nudge to find balance within, even if they aren't sure what they are trying to balance. Inner balance is a foundation for the next level of consciousness that humanity is progressively shifting toward. Here is an oversimplified view of a potential play out:

As we progressively balance our masculine and feminine energy, then our soul gets off its butt and starts releasing the gifts of our higher potentials down the pipeline to our heart. Our heart's intuitive guidance helps us use these gifts to unfold the most fulfilling version of our life. Along with this comes the compassion and desire to facilitate others to do the same.

Through countless generations, masculine energies have dominated the planet and repressed our much needed feminine qualities and sensitivity within both the male and female genders. However, that page is turning and a new one is being written. It starts the real-life chapter on the transformational benefits of balance and cooperation. Feminine energies (within men and women) are coming into their rightful, long awaited moment. More men than ever are becoming heart-vulnerable and awakening to the benefits of balancing their masculine and feminine frequencies. They are recognizing this is a missing piece in their personal empowerment process. Women are moving at god-speed in balancing these energies so that their feminine strengths and qualities can be heard, respected and equally considered. This process includes the challenge of not getting too dominant in male frequencies from over-compensation as this can create a hindrance in the personal transformation process. Staying close to the heart can help to guide and anchor this delicate balance.

Accessing our heart's intelligence can make these balancing adjustments much friendlier and more effective. As our heart and mind advance into a *partnership*, this naturally brings balance and adjustment in our masculine and feminine energies with much more ease and grace. Some people are born with more aspects of masculine/feminine balance. That wasn't me. I was a little male-heavy. In the neighborhood I was raised in as a boy, it would have been fighting words if someone had told me that I needed to wake up "the girl in me" to become a balanced person. However, my ego vanity softened through the years.

Global Rangers Skit: *"Alright men, let's saddle up and ride through the planet to straighten out this global stress mess." "Should we take the ladies?" someone shouted. "Oh, they already left in a gallop—they already sensed humanity's needs and are well on their way to assist!" "Well gentlemen, we better get moving to see if there's anything left that we can still feel like we are in charge of!"*

Ego

Our ego is not the boogie man, and with patience and inner guidance it can be transformed into its higher vibrational purpose. Qualifying life through the heart transforms the frequency of our ego nature and brings it into resonance with the vibration of our true self. For most of us, our ego in its lower vibration has created problems along the way that we've blamed on others and life. Our heart's guidance can help to bring about a natural maturing process of our ego nature at each stage of our increased awareness. This is much more effective for taming the ego than shaming it or blaming it. When I first got on the path, I would become spiritually congested from criticizing and hammering on my ego like a woodpecker, thinking I was on a fast track to self-mastery (while hoping God was watching my moves). I eventually learned that putting too much pressure on ego supervision comes from the ego itself. Our intentions to tame our ego can seem noble. Yet, if they are mind-driven intentions without the heart's deeper discernment, they create stress from constant setbacks—especially from trying to spiritually advance too quickly like the rabbit, without the wisdom and patience of the turtle.

As we commit to making peace with our ego without condemning it, then our heart's coaching will eventually transform it into the ways it serves our highest best, and in perfect timing. Don't throw your ego out with the bath water. The ego becomes transformed as it advances through the stages of reducing self-centeredness. All aspects of our nature, including our ego, are part of our divinity and play important roles in the process of becoming our empowered best. Love and appreciate them all.

Happiness

There is a lot of recent research and books written on happiness and even a country (Bhutan) that measures "Gross National Happiness." I realize it's hard not to feel that happiness is sourced from the outside—people, places and things. I embarked on an endless search to find peace and state-of-the-art happiness until I realized that my mind was searching for something that my heart was more qualified at providing. The mind is wonderful, but when it comes to deep-dive assessment regarding what will really make us happy, we are smart to engage our heart's intelligence and soul's wisdom. The mind and emotions may *pout* a little when we ask our heart's discernment to help run the show, but eventually our mind will savor the idea of having such a grounded partnership as the intelligent heart.

At times people can experience long, empty spaces between really being happy and just getting by. Opening our heart more in our interactions with others helps fill these empty spaces with care and deeper connections. This is a higher vibrational practice, and a fundamental step towards personal happiness and fulfillment. As we practice raising the vibration of our love rather than chasing happiness through people, stimulation and stuff (even if it's good stuff), we will discover that increased happiness is a natural occurrence *that just shows up when we are qualifying life through our heart.*

Happiness is a higher vibration that we often pursue from a lower vibrational attitude and we can't quite catch it by the tail. Happy periods can be extended or fragmented, based on how much lower frequency energy we process or store (such as fear, insecurity, image challenges, hurts, resentments, etc.). These lower frequency energies create predictable glitches in our natural flow of happiness. Then we try to fill the void with behaviors that spark moments of feel-good but have a short and costly shelf-life.

When we achieve a vibration of happiness that doesn't have to be baited or conditional, then everything else is an add-on, not a depend-on (which is the mother of disappointments). For example, true grounded happiness is not dependent on how well an event goes. True happiness remains if the event gets canceled or the event was uneventful. (Even if we have to breathe-out a few times to reset.)

It's counter-productive to apply for continuous happiness without clearing out lower vibrational attitudes that can't share the same space. Happiness is an inside job—which is a game changer when we discover this. View happiness as a high-end spiritual perk that we learn to unleash from within, and not make life an endless pilgrimage trying to find it.

Let's hold compassion in our hearts for the millions of people who don't have the luxury to be concerned about happiness, as they are deeply pressed in the survival mode from wars, natural disasters, starvation, abuse, etc. We can't change this picture overnight, but our love and compassion can help in ways that we can't see. No genuine love is ever wasted even if we can't always monitor and track its fine workings. Better times for the whole are unfolding—and we are the transformational engineers.

CHAPTER 10

PART 1 - CARE VS. OVERCARE
PART 2 - COMPASSION: THE NEED OF THE TIMES
By Doc Childre

As we spiritually mature into our higher potentials, increased care comes with it. Caring more is a most valid way for love to be stepped down into practical applications that would solve and prevent many problems we mechanically create and repeat.

For the next few paragraphs I'll comment on the difference between care and overcare. Overcare is when our initial feelings of care about something or someone turn into worry, anxiety and over-identification—this can escalate into emotional depletion and the obvious stress that follows. Our care is one of our highest assets but like most anything, care has a balance point; when care crosses the line into overcare, it becomes a deficit and our health bears the consequences. Balanced care nurtures us and others while overcare drains us and hinders our effectiveness, even when our intentions are good.

We know that numerous caregivers experience a high rate of energetic burnout from not being able to find the balance between care and overcare. That's understandable because balancing our care has a predictable learning curve and it's not an easy task for people who care deeply. It's part of an emotional maturing process in learning the economy of balanced care.

Below are some typical areas where overcare can overtake us at times, lowering our vibration and draining our energy. This is a standard list you may find in many books, but let's look at these through the lens of overcare.

- Work
- Relationships
- Money
- Diet
- Children
- Parents
- Health
- Past regrets
- How we look
- How we feel

- Future security
- How we will come out
- Feeling lack
- Comparisons
- What people think of us (and what we privately think of them)

Many issues on the list are often draining us at the same time and reducing our health and vitality. Then we wonder why we don't feel like our full blown self.

An excessive (obsessive) amount of overcare and emotional turbulence can also be created from trying to navigate the learning curve of new software, computers, smartphones or other "must-have" devices. *Yes, they are helpful*, but that doesn't expunge the cumulative stress deficits accrued from the anxiety of having to keep up with it all, especially if you don't have a knack for it. A balancing gesture would be to occasionally do a reality check and ask, *"Are we consumers of our technology or are we consumed by our technology?"* or *"Are we the programmers of our gadgets or are we pawns of our gadgets?"* When addiction creeps in, we become the pawns and the gadgets become our master. Finding balance in all things is a heart intelligent practice in these accelerated times, especially when technology is fixing to explode into science fiction-type potentials. Have fun but stay in charge, or you become the pawn. There's no gray.

A stealthy ingredient in overcare is its seductive power to *justify itself,* while leaving us blindsided to its energy-sapping consequences. With practice, we can cue up our intuition to alert us when *overcare* begins to invade our feelings and perceptions. The practice of identifying and deleting overcare can save a pivotal amount of energy and health risk along the way. *Eliminating overcare does not reduce our care; it strengthens the effectiveness of our care by bringing it into balance and coherent alignment with our heart.* Any time our outgoing energy is balanced, we are smarter on our feet. View overcare as a thriving emotional virus, hidden by society's unconscious agreement that overcare is okay and *not accountable.* With commitment and our heart's guidance we can free ourselves from the seductive stress that overcare and constant worry bring us.

At first, trying to distinguish the difference between balanced care and overcare can seem complicated. This is because when we are in overcare, we can tend to feel *that's when we are caring the most.* Many issues we start to care about morph into worry. Excessive worry is a classic example of when overcare is fooling us into thinking that it's *effective care.* In our heart, most of us know that free-to-roam worry eventuates into personal energy deficits and compromises our wellbeing. *(If we truly believed that worry really helped us, we would encourage our friends and children to go find a corner and "worry" whenever life's challenges come up.)* Overcare is a deeply imprinted human tendency that's handed down through each generation. It's like a virus that can only be cured through *self*-adjustment. Others can't do it for us. There's no vaccine; however we don't need one, because overcare is nothing that we can't handle with a little focus and our heart's commitment.

Dethroning the habit of overcare is doable when our intentions are sourced from a coherent partnership between our heart, mind and emotions. Including our heart's commitment provides the strength for actualizing important intentions that otherwise fizzle before they land. Our heart energy brings fortitude and resilience into our intentions, especially as our commitments start to shrink. The magic of the heart expresses itself through ease, not will and might, though the nature of the heart is mighty and a positive force that's understated.

An obvious suggestion for eliminating overcare is to practice observing and regulating our emotional expenditures. Often we get an intuitive inspiration to change and replace an old, non-supportive emotional pattern. However, *inspiration* quickly wilts like a leftover party balloon if we don't "act on it" much sooner than later. Inspiration self-sustains as we use it. As we become more skilled with this energy, we learn to move forward with our intuitive nudges while the heat from inspiration is still warm. This multiplies our potential for achieving our aim as it raises us above the vibration of our predictable resistances. Inspiration is a spirit-filled moment. It's *a packet of free energetic initiative—with a timer on it*. As we move forward with the first *nudge* of inspiration, we can beat the human tendency to waste that intuitive gift from our heart. I've found that sometimes it's many moons before certain needed inspirations return, if we miss acting on them on the first pass. It's about learning the economy of spirit.

Overcare Exercise

Observe yourself for a few days and see how often you can catch *overcare* occupying your mind and feelings regarding yourself, others or issues. When you find yourself in anxiety or distress from overcare try this exercise:

First: While breathing in a relaxed pace, pretend you are breathing through your heart or chest area and imagine calming your mind and emotions with your breath. (Calm emotions help to create a space that enables intuitive access for clearer discernment and choices when evaluating situations.)

Next: Once you've calmed your mental and emotional vibrations, then ask yourself, "What would an attitude of balanced care look like in this situation?" After you decide, imagine breathing in that new replacement attitude for a few minutes to anchor it into your system.

Repeat this exercise a few times if feelings of overcare seem amplified and determined. Approach it with *ease*, not force. With practice, you become more conscious of when you are overcaring and you can *just stop it on the spot* (in most cases) and return to being in charge of your energy.

As you practice, don't be concerned if it doesn't work every time. (You'll get plenty more chances.) Being genuine strengthens the connection with your heart's intention. This simple tool is not just for overcare; it's helpful for any stressful challenge or situation that calls for clearer discernment without the emotional override. I've found that understanding and managing *overcare* is one of the most forward-moving steps we can take in our personal transformation process.

Here are a few more things to remember in managing *overcare*:

- ☐ Overcare is stealthy; it feels normal and unaccountable.
- ☐ Overcare is deceptive because at times it feels like *when we are caring the most* (for example – worrying).

☐ Overcare can justify itself with the skill of a seasoned lawyer.

☐ Overcare is one of our mind's favorite hang-outs when we are operating in our lower frequency pitch (when our vibes are low).

Remember that worry is one of the highest contributors to overcare because it seems so "legal" and normal. *Worry* and *fear* take overcare to the extremes. We *can* reduce and change these stress producing patterns as we put our heart into it—like we tell kids to do when committing to something important.

I'll comment on fear in the next few pages because overcare unattended often grows into fear, which is the biggest collective challenge across the planet.

Addressing Fear

It's often hard to remember that we have the choice to practice emotional regulation when triggered by fear from personal matters or global concerns, such as terrorism, civil unrest, viruses, climate change, etc. Many of us have learned that our health and well-being are jeopardized if we don't practice some form of inner balance when constantly challenged by fear—whether our fear is real or not. Panic and fear put a haze around our sensible assessments and choices by numbing our higher reasoning capacity. More people are becoming tired of fear having the power to disassemble their emotional constitution and self-security. Most of us have wished to manage fear for a long time, yet often nothing changes until we step forward and put our *heart's* commitment behind our mind's intentions. We frequently engage just our mind to resolve challenges that instead require the sensitive guidance of our heart's intelligence. The mind often trips over itself while impatiently rushing toward quick-fixes, leaving a trail of setbacks and re-starts. Our heart, working in partnership with our mind, creates an intuitive draw for information or effective steps to manage fear or other unwanted behavioral patterns.

Heart-based practices for reducing fear

From experience, I have learned the importance of approaching fear with *ease* and *self-compassion* rather than with mind struggle. Impatience sent many of my fear-reducing intentions straight to the trash basket until I learned that *patience* is also a *must* for transforming fear, not an option. When our intuitive reasoning capacity becomes restricted from fear, this causes our self-security alarm to go off and creates a powerful inner distortion which we call panic, overwhelm, etc. You can reduce this by placing importance on slowing down the vibrations of your mind and emotions; this helps to reduce the charge or intensity. It can be done by slow breathing while imagining your breath entering through your heart area. An effective way to learn to manage emotional intensity is to first practice on smaller emotions such as frustration, irritation, impatience and such. Reducing mental and emotional intensity is a gateway to intuitive sensitivity for wiser choices and solutions.

You may find this suggestion helpful:

Don't try to *stop* fear; simply commit to increasingly reduce fear *a little at a time* (with ease, not push). Don't put a timer on the process. Release self-judgment or negative feelings towards your fear as this creates more resistance. Know that fear becomes more negotiable as we reduce the extra drama created in self-talk and imaginary projections with dim outcomes. I did this habitually until I realized that my mind was addicted to over-thinking the aspects of fear—trying to be too complex in assessing my feelings (boy Freud). The more we amplify fear with drama, the more we empower the fears we wish to eliminate. Most of us already know this—until the fear pops up.

Below is a practice you may already be using for managing fear and anxiety when watching the news—if news is a trigger for you.

Simply practice breathing in the feeling of calm and emotional balance while watching the news. As you breathe, see yourself maintaining care and compassion for humanity's challenges without taking on their pain and fear. This doesn't mean that you care less. Doctors, nurses and first responders to accidents maintain their care and effectiveness without over-identifying with the pain that people are experiencing. In most cases they had to practice to develop this quality, but with patience and genuine commitment any of us can develop it as well.

If the news seems too hard to deal with at times, then know that it's okay not to watch it at all. Without truly learning dispassion, many people would probably fare better by not constantly watching the news. I often choose to watch global news because it stokes the fire of my commitment to compassion for the fear and suffering experienced throughout the planet. With practice, the mind and heart can learn to process dispassion and compassion at the same time. We have to be honest with ourselves in deciding if following the news supports or compromises our wellbeing based on our individual nature and constitution. Like many issues, the news has its assets and its deficits. Use your own heart to decide what's best for you.

The practice that helped me the most to reduce fear is this: In prayer or meditation, I would visualize love from my heart streaming into my mind and into all my cells to change my old fear imprints. While breathing, I would hold a conscious intention in my heart to change my old programs of fear and anxiety into feelings of *intelligent concern* (managed-concern)—which is a much more objective and less stressful attitude than the feeling of fear.

Fear disempowers us—whereas the attitude of *intelligent concern* creates focused care that leaves us in charge and more attuned to intuitive direction. Intelligent concern is a health-conscious replacement attitude for fear. Make a heart commitment to practice befriending fear and changing the feeling to *intelligent concern* (managed-concern). This will draw a calmer response, clearer assessment and intuitive direction for responding to whatever threatens your inner or outer security. Practicing this exercise can and will help you progressively become more confident and empowered when challenged by fear, if you are patient and committed.

Practicing on less intense fears quickly strengthened my capacity to objectively shift and dissipate some of my deeper fears and anxieties. As you practice reducing and transforming fear, realize that small steps are wise steps because they create a balanced pace which draws less discouragement. Also remember to practice with patience and self-compassion, and allow for slip-ups without self-judgment and resignation. Approach it with ease, without urgency and self-doubt.

These few paragraphs don't come close to addressing the endless situations and circumstances that can trigger our fears. People have searched for ages trying to find that "fix all, fear-eraser." Many helpful instructions are available if you research the books and information on this subject. If you desire it from your heart, you will draw information that can help you replace your fears with increased self-security.

Helping Children Maintain their Heart Connection

Often when small kids are distressed, unhappy or experiencing a tantrum, we instinctively re-direct their energy by giving them a toy or loving attention and almost instantly, they can totally change their frequency pitch (vibration) to calmness, joy, elation or contentment (higher pitch emotions). A primary reason that children often transform compressive emotions quickly is because in their early years of development they are still connected to the higher frequencies of their natural heart attributes, such as uncomplicated love, transparency, lack of prejudice, and their super-power *to release and move on.* Their minds are not yet entrained to the countless lower vibration societal mind-sets and habits that often overshadow their heart's higher feelings and choices.

The collective consciousness is slowly awakening to the need to educate children in how to maintain the connection with the natural, higher vibration of *who they really are*. This is done by helping them sustain a balanced alignment between their mind and heart as they mature. It's especially important for children to maintain connection with their heart's guidance amidst society's hard and fast entrainment in overstimulation, ambition, competition and techno-mania.

One of the biggest obstructions in a child's development (but not intentional) is when parents assume that they always know best regarding what their kids should be and do as they become adults. Millions of children end up playing out the dreams of their parent's ideal personifications. To most parents in these situations it seems normal and motivated by care. It is care—but often overcare or uneducated care which unintentionally force-fits children into molds that don't fit. Guidance is important, yet guidance occasionally needs an awareness upgrade that's more inclusive of the consequences it generates. Most everyone realizes that for a long time now, children around the world are born with more awareness than previous generations. This increased awareness can cause resistance and separation in teens when they are pressured in directions that their deeper heart feels are not right for them—especially regarding vocation and relationship choices.

There are updated guidance models that can prevent much stress and emotional suffering in children from spirit repression. Guidance needs to include an awareness of their individual nature and their deeper heart's inclinations and desires. New consciousness regarding this is on the rise, yet there's much left to be done to change old-school guidance patterns.

With compassion, I encourage parents to be proactive in becoming more informed about updated and effective new models and information regarding this subject. Most parents are doing the best they can based on their awareness and means. But it's time to upgrade our awareness because in our heart of hearts, we want our children and young adults to become *who they truly are*. Parents also need to have compassion for themselves as keeping up with children's accelerated awareness is one of the harder challenges of these times. I compassionately understand the extra commitment this takes. As we collectively desire and envision an awareness upgrade from the heart, it will come about. The sun can already be seen coming over the hill. Our younger generation's increasing awareness will eventually bail out society's conflicting lower vibrational mindsets that have cost so many lives and generated ongoing hatred, separation and retribution. They won't tend to support this ever-long impasse or tolerate the old ways that block harmonious connection and caring interactions among all people. This is all part of the consciousness shift we are experiencing.

Part 2 - Compassion: The Need of the Times

Compassion increases in effectiveness as we mature in the core qualities of the heart, such as unconditional love, allowance, acceptance and an unattached desire for the highest outcome for all concerned. Cultivating these heart qualities strengthens our compassion and frees it to serve the highest best. True compassion benefits the sender and receiver, though we can't always see the ways it nurtures and heals. Many of us have felt drained and stressed on occasion from what we thought was *giving compassion*. This energy drain and depletion come mostly from unbalanced empathetic care. Empathy can produce strong feelings of care but often comes with tentacles that create over-attachment to what we care about.

Compassion is one of the highest supportive energies of love. I used to think it was for fixing others. We can support each other with our love and compassion but people have to do their own mending from within. I was a dedicated "Mr. Fix-all" until I learned that people have to do their own fixing or similar challenges keep repeating—sometimes in different arrangements, and sometimes in much harder circumstances. Often the problems we rush to fix for others are their growth opportunities for learning to connect more deeply within their own heart and soul for direction and solutions.

Learning to *balance* our empathetic interactions is a big step towards understanding the tone of true compassion. It's an unconditional love that supports the highest outcome for others without depleting our personal reservoir of energy. Whereas unmanaged empathy, sympathetic attachment, and "tired-care" are the rocks to look behind when we feel drained from extending what we felt was our heart's compassion. One reason that compassion is misunderstood is that for ages, people have used the term *compassion* as a convenient *cover-all word* for what is often sympathy, empathy, pity or excessive worry. More people are being prompted from within to gain a deeper understanding of compassion, since compassion tops the list of what would benefit humanity in these transitional times.

Compassion is a powerful core frequency within our heart, but in most cases it takes practice to feel love and care for people in extreme stress without becoming overly identified with their challenges (a learning curve for all of us). One expression of true compassion is when we can hold love and light for others in dark moments, without draining our own battery and joining them in the dark. As we balance and manage our care we increase the effectiveness of our compassion. Without balance, our attempts to be compassionate turn into overcare and result in an energy deficit.

More about Empathy

The following is similar in ways to the content on compassion. But since compassion is so often confused with empathy, I feel it could be helpful to restate a few points that set these two expressions of care apart. As I mentioned earlier, sensitivity to other's pain points often triggers feelings of compassion and empathetic care; yet our effectiveness diminishes rapidly when we over-attach emotionally to their issues. Compassion can sense the suffering of others, yet can maintain balance and energetic composure within its care.

News stories, children's challenges, other people's health issues, etc. can elicit our empathetic responses which, without management, can trigger a continuous drain throughout our whole system, even if we feel like we are "kind of in charge." Empathy starts out as an asset, yet it can become a misery if we don't find our balance with it. A reality moment is when we realize (not just intellectually, but *really* get it) that unmanaged empathy can produce continuous energy deficits that far out-weigh the "good" which we think we are providing. Unnecessary aging comes with this package.

The following is a standard outcome that most of us have read about or experienced from unmanaged empathy:

*On the edge of burnout, we end up livid with ourselves for sinking too deep into others' challenges, or the world's problems, and then we get angry because there's nobody to blame but ourselves (though we give it a good try). It gets worse as we remember that we learned our lesson the last time this happened—and here we are again. This is often followed by self-judgment and self-reduction until we get too worn down to even do that. Then we stressfully re-gather ourselves over a period of time and start all over with new self-care commitments, feeling like we've **really** learned our lesson this time...*

We can change the ending to these self-generated stress ambushes by paying more attention to the intuitive feelings that signal us when our care becomes imbalanced—when our empathetic care fades into *over-care, attachment and self-depletion.* Our heart's intelligence often provides intuitive warnings before self-depletion sets in but we can fall short on taking action, often because we think our overcare is justified. At times our mind diverts us from our heart's choices when our ego pouts because it wants something different. Ego is good at seizing the moment when our intentions are rickety and not anchored in the heart. Our ego will surrender to the strength of our inner dignity once it senses our commitment is heart-solid.

Like many others, my heart intuition was blocked by my mind's misinterpretation of empathy. I thought living on the edge of burnout from serving others was virtuous and noble. I felt it was proof of my self-sacrifice "to share the light and spread the good" like a little knight. (Picture a knight in shining ignorance on a mission to *fix everyone*, whatever the personal cost—that was me at age twenty-five.) Much of that experience was from young-buck ego vanity, mixed with sincere, yet *unbalanced* care. I've moved on since then after learning the same lesson, repeatedly. But I still closely monitor the difference between empathy and balanced care. It stays high on my personal list of self-care maintenance practices.

Remember, empathy itself is not the source of energy drains; it's the unintentional mishandling of this ability that drains and taxes our wellbeing. Our hearts have the capacity to maintain energetic detachment and emotional equability. It's one of the most valuable gifts we can give ourselves. Balanced empathy can nurture and serve others without serving us up with it. Learning the difference between lower empathetic attachment and balanced care can help dissolve most of the problems around empathy, and help us mature in the understanding of true compassion and its effectiveness.

This practice may be helpful in balancing empathy:

Practice watching some recorded movie scenes where the characters are experiencing a medium amount of physical or emotional pain that creates a challenging sympathetic or empathetic feeling in you. As you watch, imagine you are breathing through your heart space, or the center of your chest. Breathe in a relaxed way and practice detaching yourself from the emotional over-identification.

If you do this enough times you will eventually find a place within yourself where you can regulate your feelings. You will start to realize that you can actually care about what is going on without it pulling you into it. The advantage of repeating the scenes is that it gives you more chances in a row to experiment with finding that *inner switch* which regulates your emotional output. Practicing with movie scenes gives you a jump start on learning dispassion and intentional composure which help with learning true compassion. These types of practices are often used by first responders to learn to maintain emotional composure as they respond to car wrecks, catastrophes, and such. This skill can be developed. Know in your heart that maintaining your emotional composure, without suffering with people in distress, doesn't mean that you care less for them. Your care and compassion are actually more effective.

Self-Compassion

Self-compassion is an advanced step in anyone's personal empowerment and self-care maintenance practices. At first people tend to respond awkwardly when it's suggested they feel compassion for themselves—it can seem a little self-serving, out of place, undeserved, un-spiritual, etc. These attitudes come from handed-down entrainment from old belief systems that don't serve us anymore. Self-compassion has been on the back-burner too long, and now it's time to seize the moment and take advantage of its transformational benefits. To have compassion for yourself is not an act of selfishness; it's an act of intelligence, heart intelligence.

Don't confuse self-compassion with pity-party type emotions; it's a transformative vibration from our heart that nurtures us with a non-judgmental acceptance and a deeper understanding of our self. Practicing this form of self-care (love) is especially helpful when transitioning through situations that require time for healing and emotional adjustment. If we have physical or emotional challenges, self-compassion intuitively guides and supports us through the best ways to handle our issues or situations. However, self-compassion is not just for challenging times as it could seem. Self-compassion is a regenerative energy that serves as a tonic for our cells and our operating system.

Self-compassion is a higher vibrational frequency sourced from the love and power of our heart and soul. We obviously think compassion is beneficial or else we wouldn't automatically gush it out to others, pets, world suffering, etc. Why wouldn't we do this for ourselves—love is love and it does what it does, and it's free. So don't feel awkward about a little self-love. Compassionate self-love is not ego infatuation. It's an intelligent and regenerative self-maintenance practice.

To practice self-compassion simply get quiet somewhere and imagine creating an inner spa. Imagine breathing self-compassion into your mental/emotional nature and into your physical cells. Do this for a while—like a meditation. Most importantly, do this from the heart as it connects directly with the renewing qualities of your soul vibration. As you become familiar with the practice, it will begin to feel as if you are interacting with a best friend who truly cares, understands and supports.

....

Compassion is a most powerful and intelligent frequency within the love spectrum. As we unconditionally express compassion, it intuitively chooses its own way to administer its care—based on a sensitive attunement to the higher need of the whole. Pure compassion is not tethered to our agendas; it's free to weave its magic, sometimes visibly yet often unseen, but never wasted as it nurtures all within its radiance. True compassion supports the highest-best outcome, which is not always what our personality would choose or under-

stand. Unconditional love sets the tone for compassion, distinguishing it from lower vibrational attachments which hinder effectiveness. As our human intelligence spirals to the next station of enlightenment, then collective compassion will become the foundational vibration for amplifying the connection with our soul and source as they stream love and healing through our human experience. Compassion is transformational love and care manifesting in the most ripened state of effectiveness for the whole. – Doc

CHAPTER 11

HEART-BASED LIVING
By Doc Childre

In this book, our intention has been to provide research and understandings about the "heart" as a dynamic, unifying, creative intelligence. A coherent alignment between our spiritual heart, mind and emotions can lead to a new way of perceiving, thinking, and relating which we call *heart-based living*.

Heart-based living is a natural self-maintenance, self-transformational practice. It begins with each one of us, by befriending the intuitive guidance within our heart and bringing it forward into how we conduct our lives day-to-day. Our heart's intelligence can offer us, personally and collectively, a chance to create (not wait for) our fulfillment. With genuine practice, we can find within our heart the answers and directions for the next steps along our path to becoming our empowered, true self.

Our heart's intuitive feelings and discernment regarding life's issues are natural gifts that we can refer to, no matter what religion, personal growth, or spiritual path we may believe in or practice. We don't have to be on a particular path to experience the limitless benefits of our heart's intelligent directions. My approach is that of *practical spirituality*—such as the practice of integrating love, kindness and compassion into our daily interactions with others, and allowing for differences without creating separation.

The accelerating changes of these times offer us increased opportunities to advance in consciousness—by integrating our spiritual heart's wisdom with our human intelligence into a *oneness* relationship. The continuous availability of new information is helping humanity to realize we are all connected, and that caring for others and ourselves is caring for the whole. More people are prompted from within to be kinder with each other. These times are lit with positive opportunity regardless of how it can appear throughout the planet.

People all over the globe are talking about and practicing compassion. There are "compassion centers" being created at universities and other locations. Compassion (and self-compassion) is a higher vibrational feeling sourced from the love and wisdom of our heart and soul.

People are becoming more sensitive to their heart's promptings to care more, not just for the sake of being good, but because it's intelligent and harmonizes the energetic environment. More people are practicing meditation to find inner stillness and to release identification with thoughts and attitudes that no longer serve who they want to become.

Increasing numbers are exploring a deeper connection with their heart's feelings and guidance for the reason that nothing else seems to fulfill certain empty spaces in their life. Many are sensing that the heart is a natural intuitive conduit to their soul's love and assistance.

Accessing our heart's intuitive intelligence for discerning choices and directions will eventually be accepted as practical common sense. As more of humanity practices heart-based living (or heart-centered living), it will help qualify the "rite of passage" into a next level of consciousness and intelligence. We have offered in this book a few heart intelligent strategies and exercises that we have found helpful. There are many effective tools nowadays for supporting an upgrade to our higher potentials, and our heart's intuition can guide us to them in perfect timing.

About Coherence

Coherence occurs at all levels in nature, from the micro to the macro, and within the human experience. While in a heart coherent state we experience a distinct quieting of the inner "noise" generated by the normal stream of unregulated mental and emotional activity; we have a greater sense of alignment as well as a stronger connection with our heart's intuitive feelings or inner guidance.

Heart coherence does not disesteem the mind; it increases our mind's potentials and helps it expand into balanced viewpoints that are more inclusive of the whole. Our basic systems (heart, mind, emotions and body) create more harmony and fulfillment when working in partnership to shape our lives. The practice of sitting in heart coherence accumulates higher vibrational energy that has a carryover effect through our day; it provides more clarity in discernment and ability to access flow. This often draws creative solutions where there seem to be none. In a coherent vibration we draw more synchronicities and clearer choices, along with heightened heart textures of love in our life's interactions. We don't have to be perfect without challenges to maintain a coherent life expression. It simply requires general maintenance, like any practice which deals with influences that steer our decisions and behaviors. Coherence is a natural state that accompanies who we are at the core of our being.

Scientific research is also indicating that as people practice heart coherence, it generates an energetic field that makes it easier for others to connect with their heart—facilitating *social coherence*. It's our job to become responsible for our energy, which raises the vibration of the collective energy field, making it easier for others to access their higher potentials and increased joy. The emerging field of interconnectivity research is exploring how this higher vibration can be amplified, creating the potential for *global coherence.* As collective awareness increases, science and spiritual exploration will join together in partnership which will create unlimited benefits for the whole of humanity. A higher vibration of unconditional love and non-judgment stands to become the new baseline for increased coherence, harmony and cooperation between our own heart and mind, with each other, and with Earth.

Unconditional Love

As collective consciousness increases, this will eventually reveal that love is an advanced mode of intelligent living. People have just scratched the surface of awareness regarding the focused power of love and its capacity to create a heart-based environment; one where individuals can transcend fear and what it brings, while manifesting their undiscovered gifts and fulfillment. Unconditional love is the next vibration of love that humanity is transitioning into and this will eliminate much of the standard complications and problems that seem to form around love's powerful transformational energy.

The increasing influence of the collective heart opening will help dissipate humanity's darker cloud covers. As the heart opens, this creates the long awaited opportunity for humanity to start getting along with each other and allow a budding renaissance of enlightenment and increased fulfillment to unfold.

One aspect of the HeartMath mission is to work in alignment with other systems whose intention is to increase harmony, kindness and compassion throughout the planet. Millions of people are participating in collective prayer, meditation and compassion initiatives to affect a higher outcome for our planet. I suggest that this won't be a passing trend; it will become a common sense practice for the good of the whole. The effectiveness of these outpourings will increase as participants' coherence increases, which raises the collective vibration. It's this higher vibration of our spirit that creates the benevolent outcomes, more so than the numbers of people involved—yet numbers help, especially as people increase their personal coherence. As our heart, mind and emotions resonate in coherent alignment, this allows more spirit and heart energy into our individual and collective intentions. The collective intention for the Global Coherence Initiative is to help bring about this transforming environment, however long it takes. Many people throughout the planet are practicing coherent alignment to unlock their higher potentials and free up the spirit of who they truly are.

It's time to realize that powerful, life changing positive movements are growing in the midst of the transitional chaos that the planet is going through. More people are sensing that some of the rough edges humanity is experiencing are the release of old energies that no longer serve us, which creates an opportunity to *reset our lives.* As a result of these energetic changes, people will progressively wake up and recognize (not just quote) that we can become much more than we ever thought possible—yet we have to individually pedal some to create that ride.

Our present global situation is not the same as a storm where we bunker down and wait it out, and then back to business as usual. The ball is in our court, as we are all players in the outcome. The global intensities won't last forever. For now, we can view the chaos and unrest as neon signs which indicate it's time to open our hearts, grab our toolbox and techniques, and make some needed changes for the better. In doing so, we are repurposing the global stress and uncertainty into a positive momentum to get us off the couch. Love, compassion, kindness and cooperation have been sparsely represented in our collective social consciousness for too long. Let's place these transformative heart qualities on the top shelf of our toolbox as we pitch in to co-create the highest best future for the whole. I feel that being kinder and more compassionate to each other is the best kept secret for quickening the advancement of humanity. As we do this, the rest of what we need will follow. Accessing our natural heart intelligence *can* create an energetic field of unconditional love and harmonious interaction—helping humanity to realize we are one Earth, one yard, one people. Love is the one thing that can bring all this together coherently and eventually thrive.

Many of us have committed to *giving peace a chance* but peace is waiting on us to take the first responsible step: Now it's time *to give love a chance*—then peace will join us at the table for celebration.

ABOUT THE AUTHORS

**Doc Childre,
HeartMath Founder,
Chairman and Co-CEO**

Doc is the founder of HeartMath and a global authority on optimizing human performance and personal effectiveness and a consultant to business leaders, scientists, educators and the entertainment industry. He is the originator of the HeartMath® System, a set of practical, heart-based tools and technologies that all people can use to reduce stress, improve performance, and enhance health and well-being. He is Chairman and co-CEO of HeartMath, Inc., and Chairman of HeartMath Institute's Scientific Advisory Board and Global Coherence Initiative Steering Committee.

Deborah Rozman, Ph.D., HeartMath Inc. President and Co-CEO

Deborah has over forty years of experience as a business executive, serial entrepreneur, psychologist, author, and educator. She has been involved with HeartMath since its inception helping to oversee its growth. She is co-author with Doc Childre of HeartMath's Transforming Series published by New Harbinger: *Transforming Stress, Transforming Anger, Transforming Anxiety and Transforming Depression*, and is a key spokesperson on HeartMath, heart intelligence, managing stress in changing times and heart-based living.

Howard Martin, HeartMath LLC Executive Vice President

Howard brings more than thirty years of experience in business and personal development and has been involved in the development of HeartMath's programs since its inception. He is co-author with Doc Childre of *The Heart-Math Solution*, published in 2000 by Harper San Francisco. Howard is a key spokesperson conducting over 75 interviews each year and speaking internationally on the HeartMath approach to advancing human performance, global coherence and heart intelligence.

Rollin McCraty, Ph.D., HeartMath Institute, Executive Vice President and Director of Research

Rollin has been with HeartMath since its creation in 1991. He is a psychophysiologist and a professor at Florida Atlantic University. He has written extensively and been widely published in his areas of scientific interest. He holds numerous memberships, including with the American Autonomic Society, Pavlovian Society, National Association for Psychological Science, Association for Applied Psychophysiology and Biofeedback and Society for Scientific Exploration and is director of research and project coordinator of the Global Coherence Monitoring System.

ADDITIONAL RESOURCES

HeartMath LLC

Connect with Us

Sign-up for our *Heartfully Speaking* e-newsletter.
Join our growing community of like-hearted people on
Facebook.com/HeartMath
Find us on Linked-In at
linkedin.com/company/heartmath-llc

Daily Practice

Our Inner Balance and emWave technology products
are designed to help individuals connect deeper with
their heart intelligence. These award-winning technologies are fun to use and can guide you into a deeper,
more connected state of heart coherence through real-
time heart rhythm feedback and training.

Welcome Gift!

Use coupon code **HeartIntell25** with your first purchase from the store.heartmath.com. Get $25.00 off a
purchase of $100.00 or more. (*Offer expires 11/1/16,*

cannot be combined with other offers or applied to past purchases.)

Become a Champion of Heart Intelligence

<u>Coaches and Mentors</u> – Our team of HeartMath Certified Coaches and Mentors are trained and licensed to teach clients the HeartMath System in a one-on-one and small group settings.

<u>HeartMath Interventions</u> - HeartMath Interventions Program is uniquely designed for doctors, nurses, psychologists, licensed therapists, counselors, social workers, and other health professionals who want to add HeartMath tools and technologies into their therapeutic work with clients or patients.

<u>HeartMath Certified Trainers</u> - The HeartMath® Certified Trainer program provides organizational and independent trainers and consultants with the training and license to deliver the Resilience Advantage^{TM}, a best-in-class program used by the US Navy, hospital systems and Fortune 500 companies world-wide.

How to contact us:
<u>HeartMath.com</u>
<u>info@heartmath.com</u>
P.O. Box 1463

Boulder Creek, California 95006
800-450-9111
(831) 338-8700
HeartMath Institute

Become a HeartMath Institute (HMI) Member

HeartMath Institute members enjoy perks such as e-books, scientific monographs, e-music, informative webinars created exclusively for members and unlimited access to an array of resources. You'll also have easy access to your free resources on your personalized My Member Page, where you can stay informed and be enriched and inspired on your journey of the heart.

Donate

Your charitable gift to HeartMath Institute supports innovative research in heart rate variability (HRV), the psychophysiology of emotions, heart-brain communication and how these relate to managing stress, increasing coherence and deepening your connection to self and others. HMI's research has led to the development of effective programs and simple techniques for increasing personal, social and global coherence and harmony. Your generosity improves the lives of children, adults and those in need. It enables HMI to continue exploring two of our most exciting areas of research: the electrophysiology of intuition and the interconnectedness of all things. HeartMath Institute is a "100% model," meaning all contributions support research and projects that help people.

Support HeartMath Education Projects

Teaching children how to access their hearts' wisdom is essential for creating a heart-based world and future. Learning emotional awareness and self-regulation skills early in life greatly increases the likelihood for future success. Social and behavioral science show these critical skills underlie mental and emotional health, positive relationships and success in school. HeartMath's nearly 25 years of research is incorporated in practical tools and programs that give parents, teachers and other educators skills to help children attain these skills and fully engage in life. Your charitable gift to HeartMath Education Projects provides sponsorships for life-changing educational programs and resources to students, teachers and those who otherwise could not access them.

Resources for Building Heart Intelligence

Resources to Empower You

Explore HeartMath's collection of free resources and downloadable materials for expanding your heart connections. These include practical solutions for personal growth, health and life fulfillment.

Stress & Well-Being Survey

This scientifically developed assessment tool guides you, whenever you need it, in determining the state of your heart, mind and emotions at home, at work and in your relationships and finances. It measures your stress management, adaptability, resilience and emotional vitality. The survey analyzes the data in relation to 5 Aspects of well-being and makes recommendations.

Resources for Heart-Coherent Parenting

Visit our resources page for parents, where you'll find many articles covering a range of topics, ideas and tools for those who raise children. You'll also find parenting self-care resources to help you take care of your needs so you can take care of your children's.

Connect with HeartMath Institute

Join our growing community on <u>Face-book.com/InstituteofHeartMath.</u>

Find us on Linked-In at

<u>linkedin.com/company/institute-of-heartmath.</u>

Check out our <u>blog</u>.

HeartMath.org

<u>info@heartmath.org</u>

P.O. Box 1463

Boulder Creek, California 95006

(800) 711-6221

(831) 338-8500